W9-CIF-477

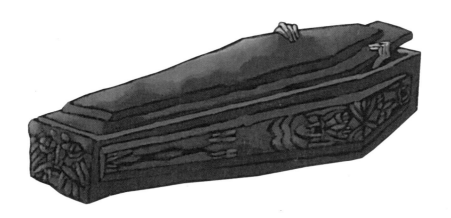

ALBERTO
BRECCIA'S
Dracula

Contents

The Last Night of Carnival

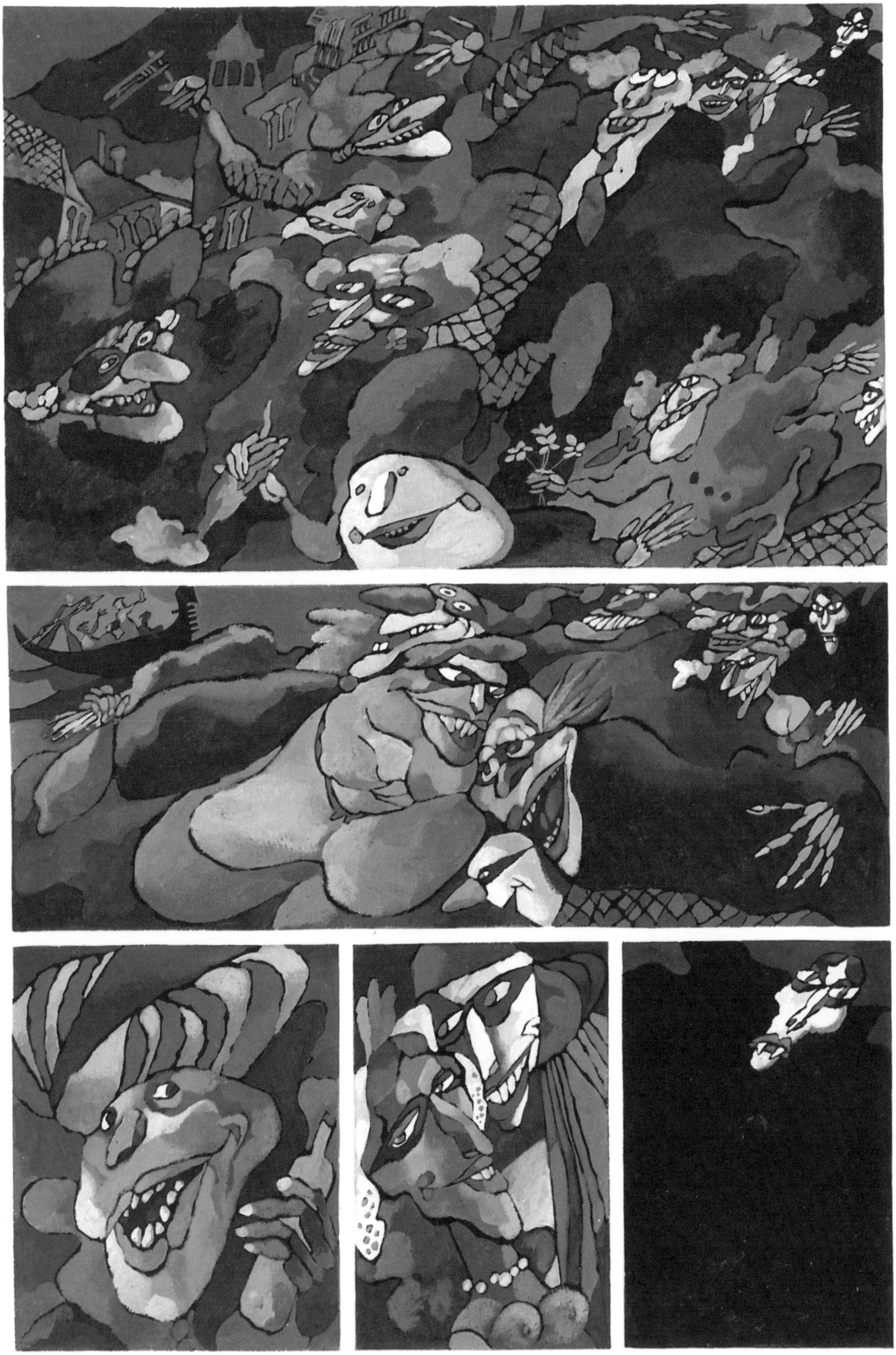

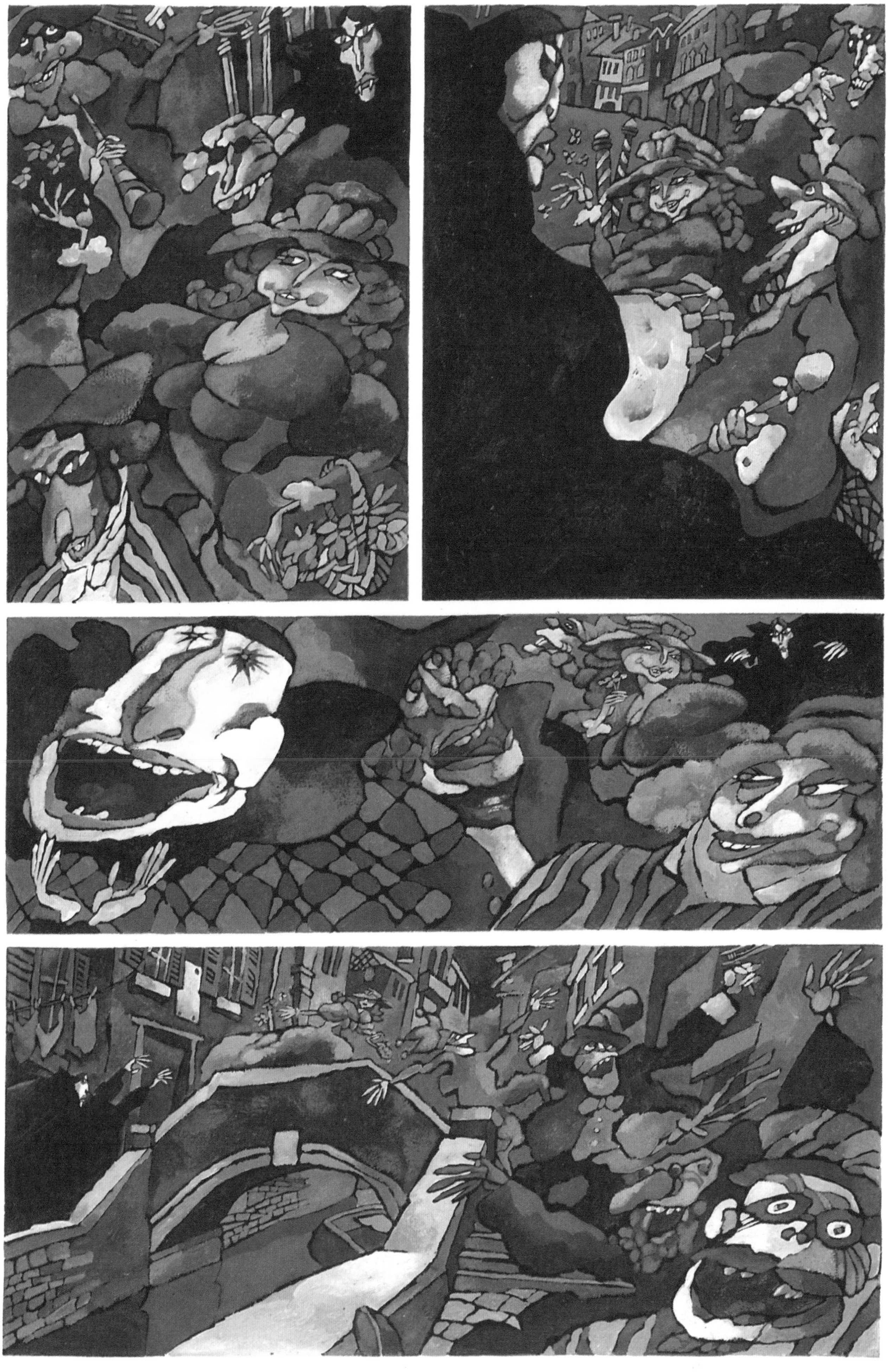

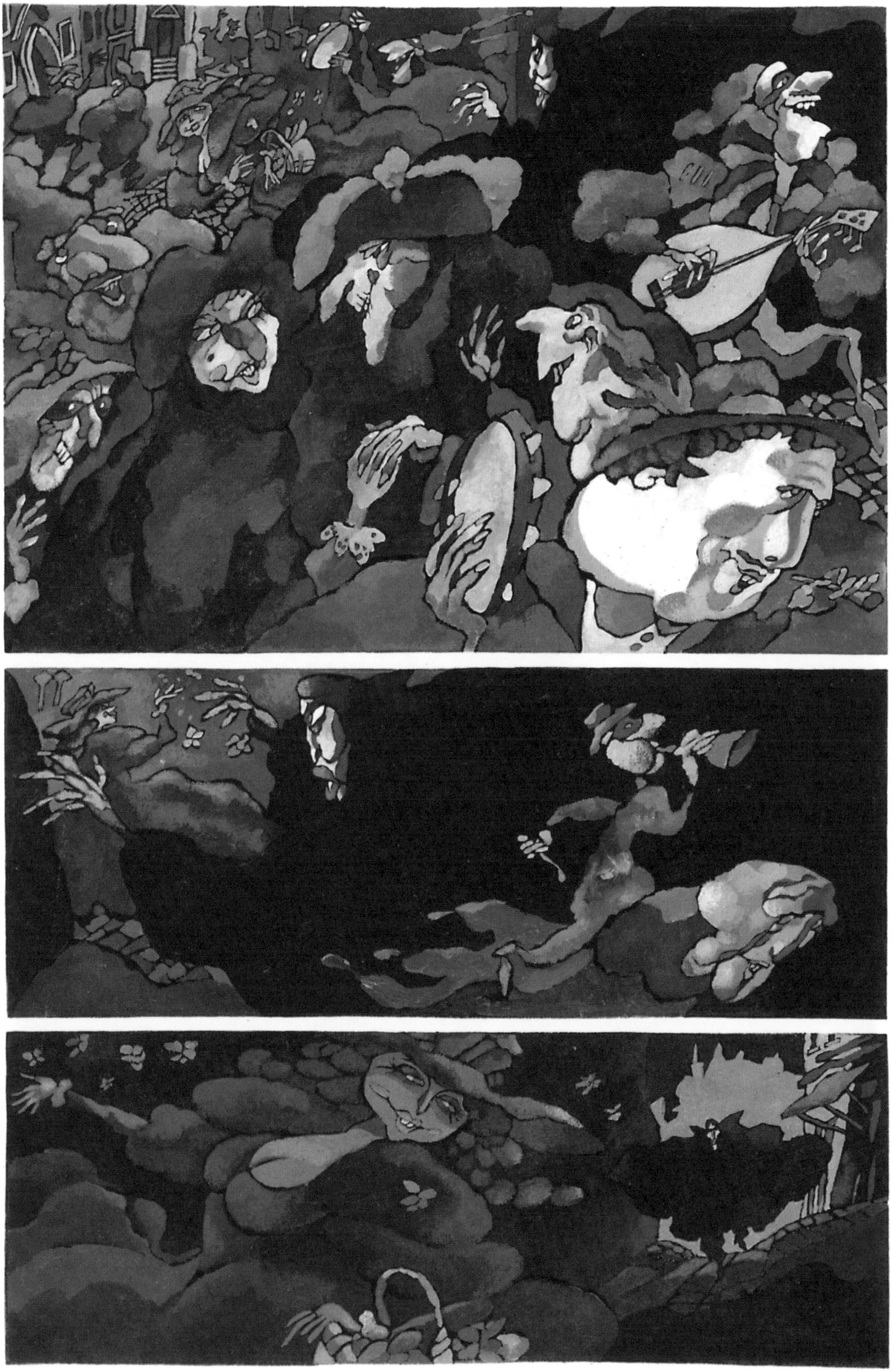

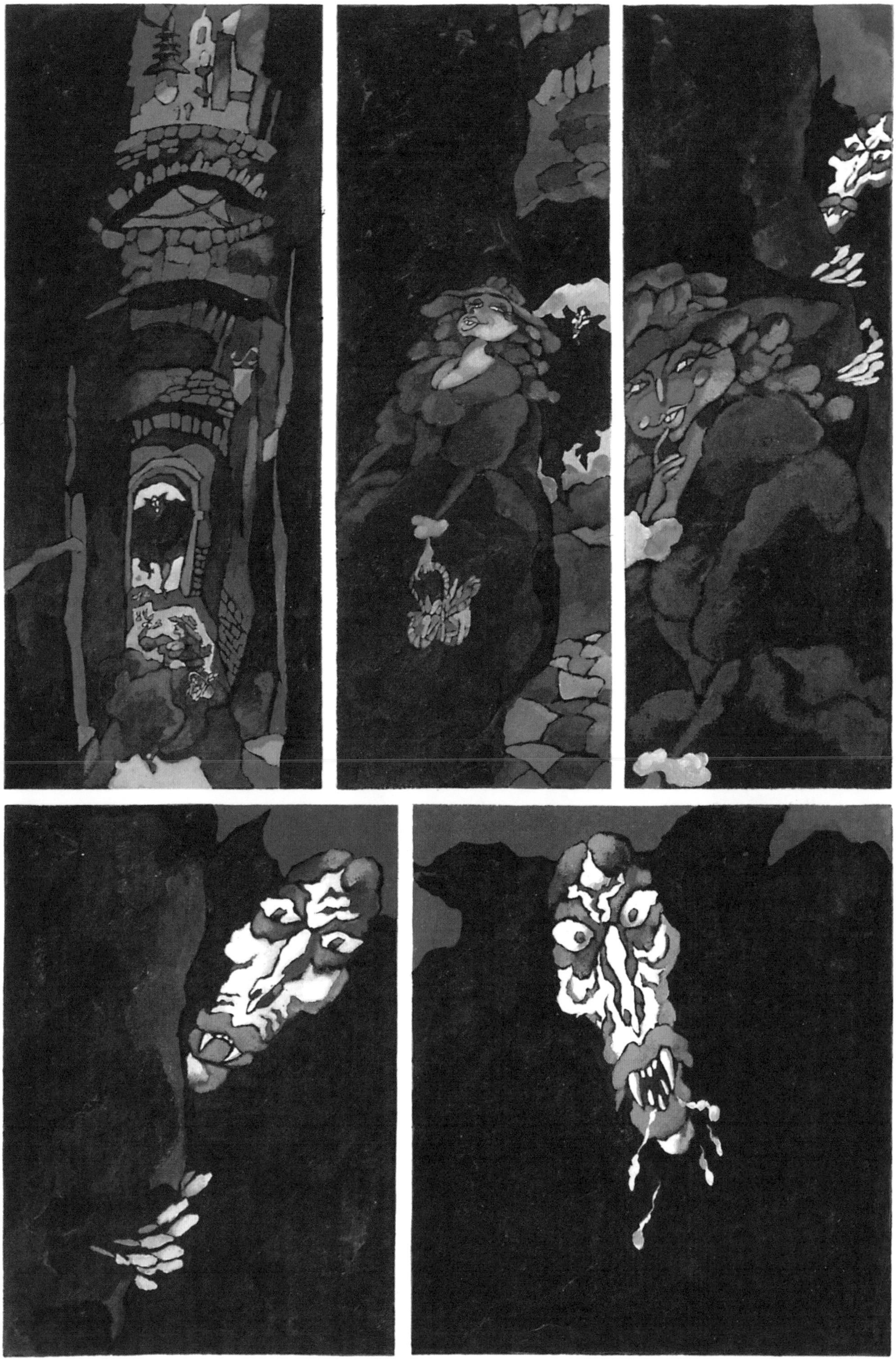

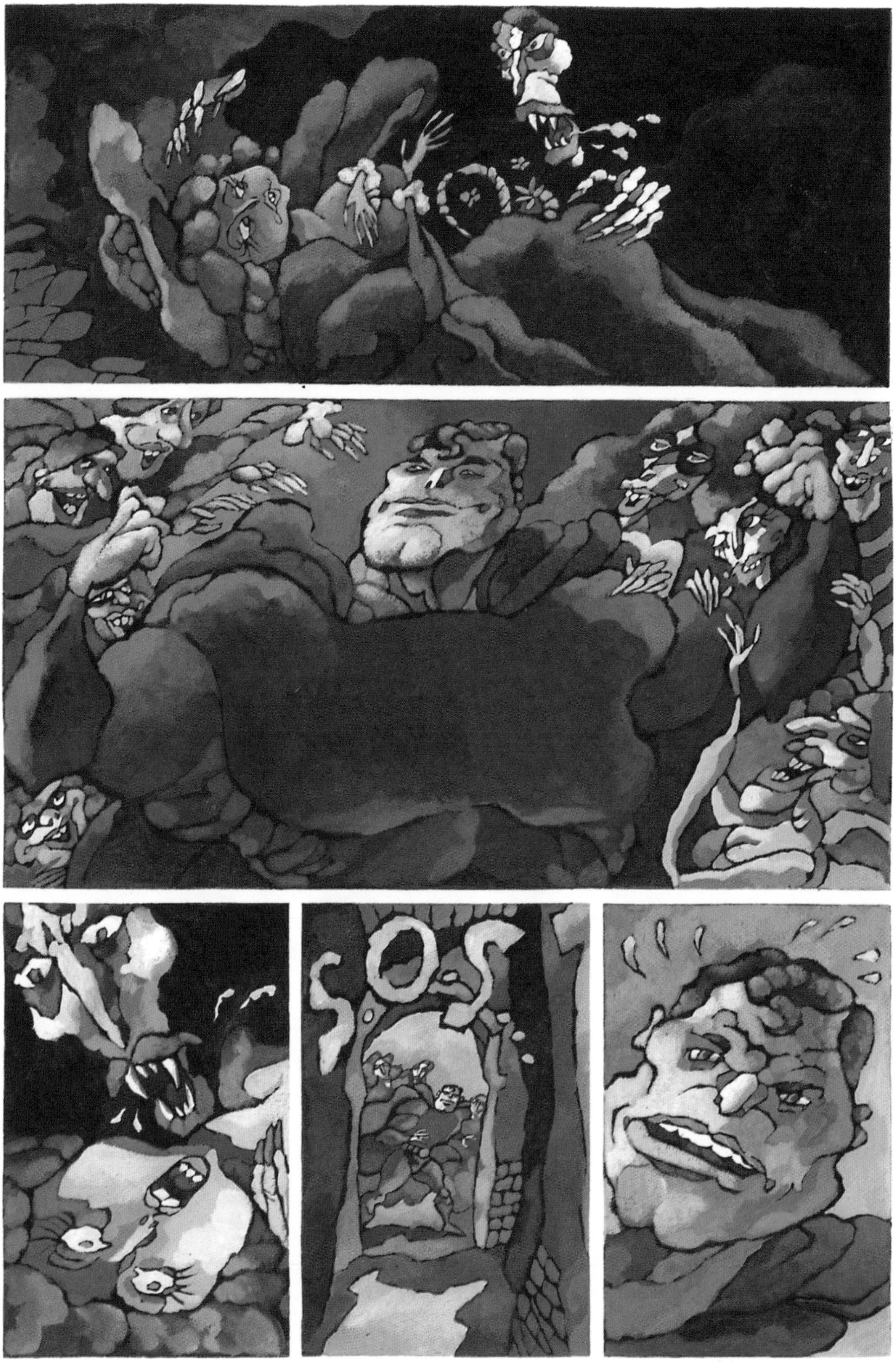
SOS

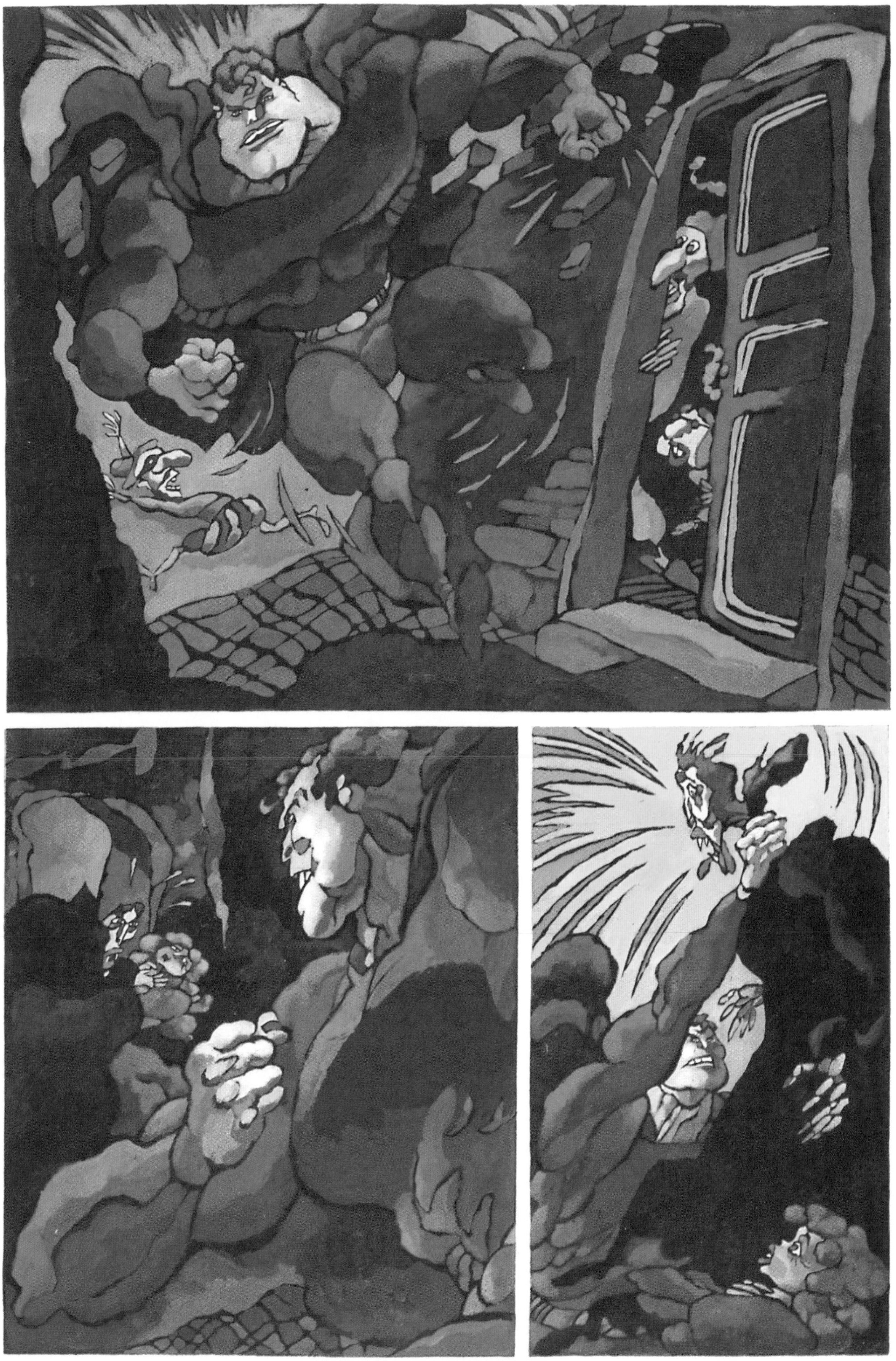

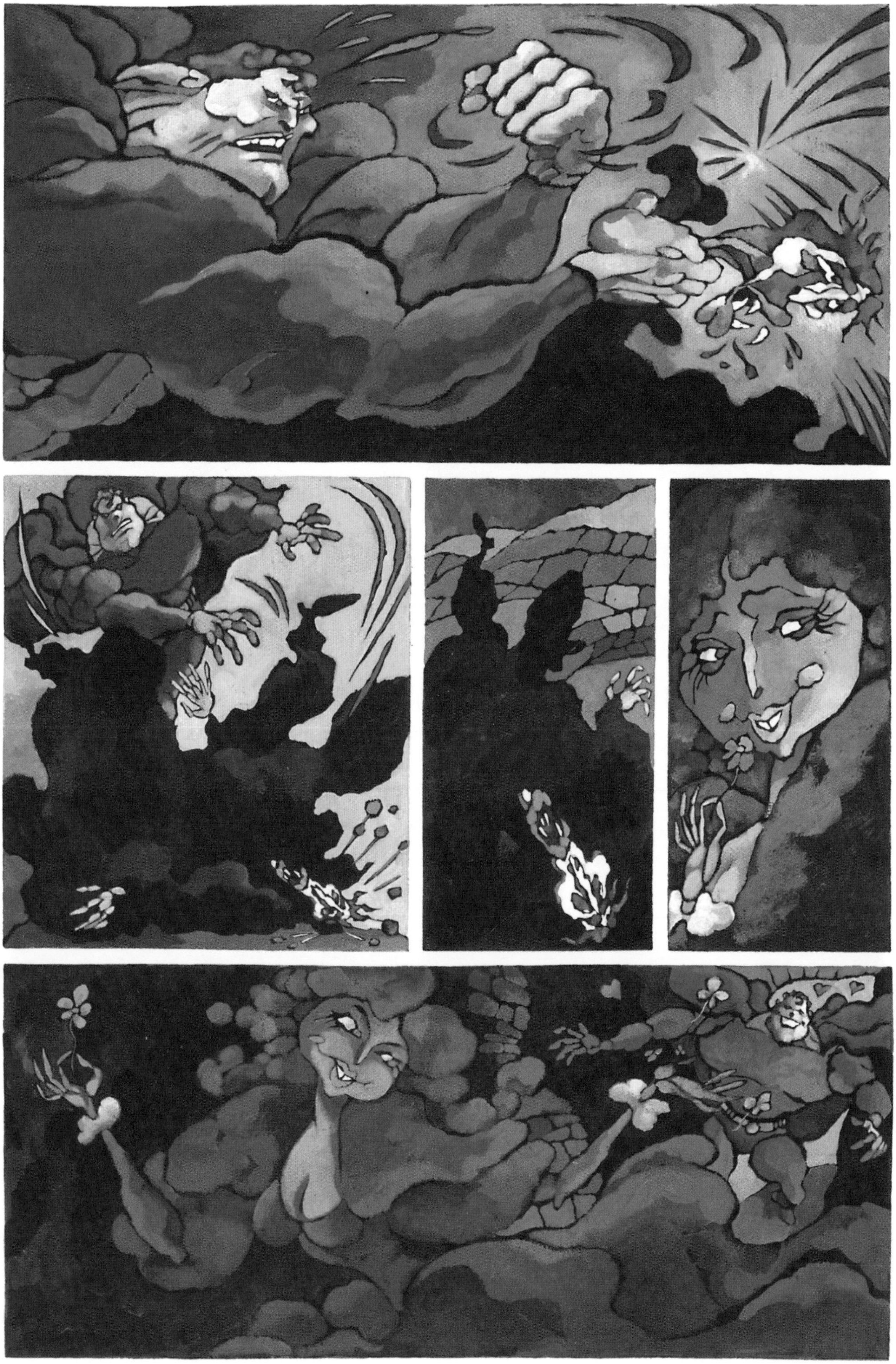

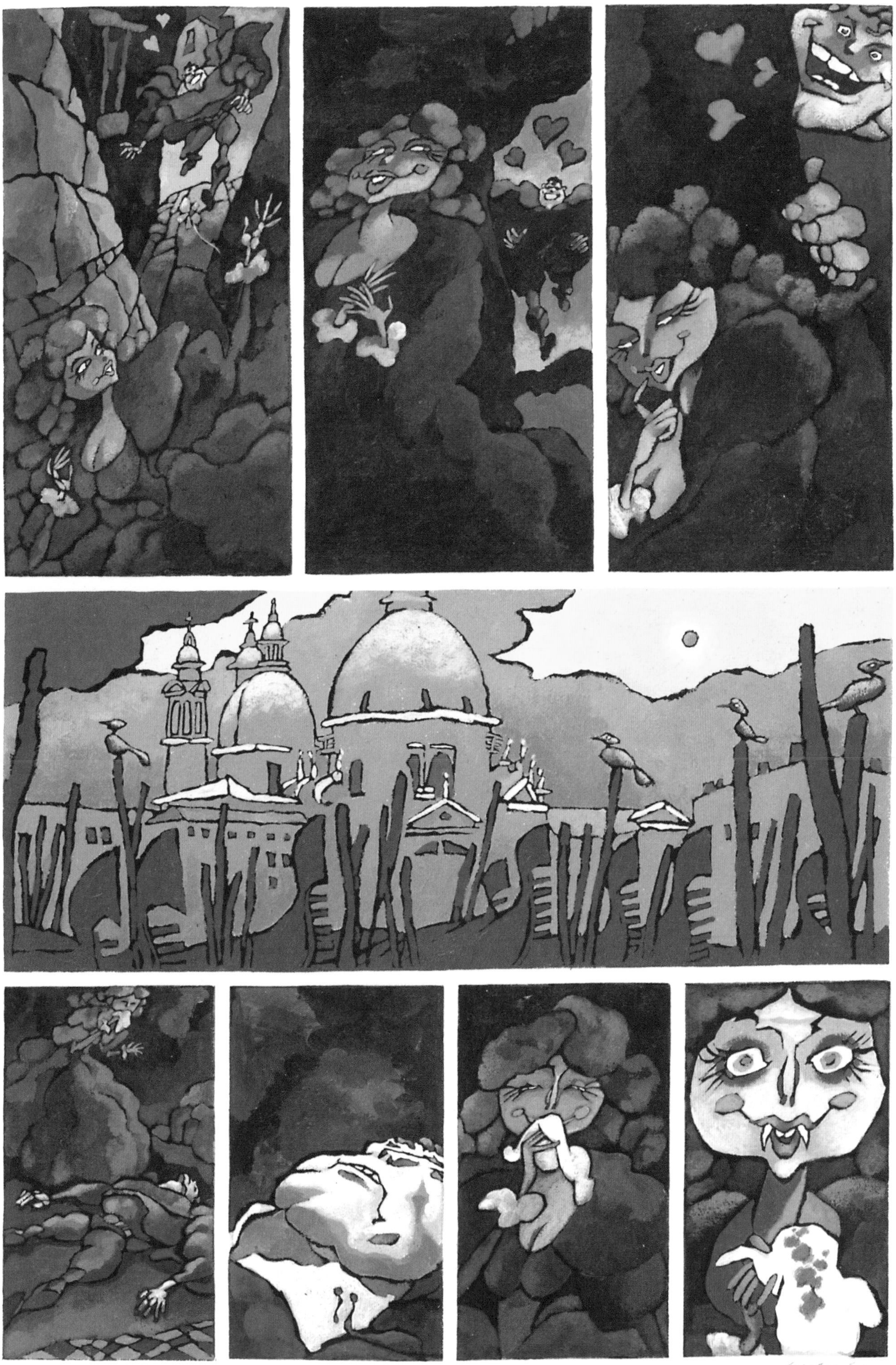

TWO

Latrans canis non admordet*

*A Barking Dog Never Bites,
or: His Bark Is Worse than His Bite

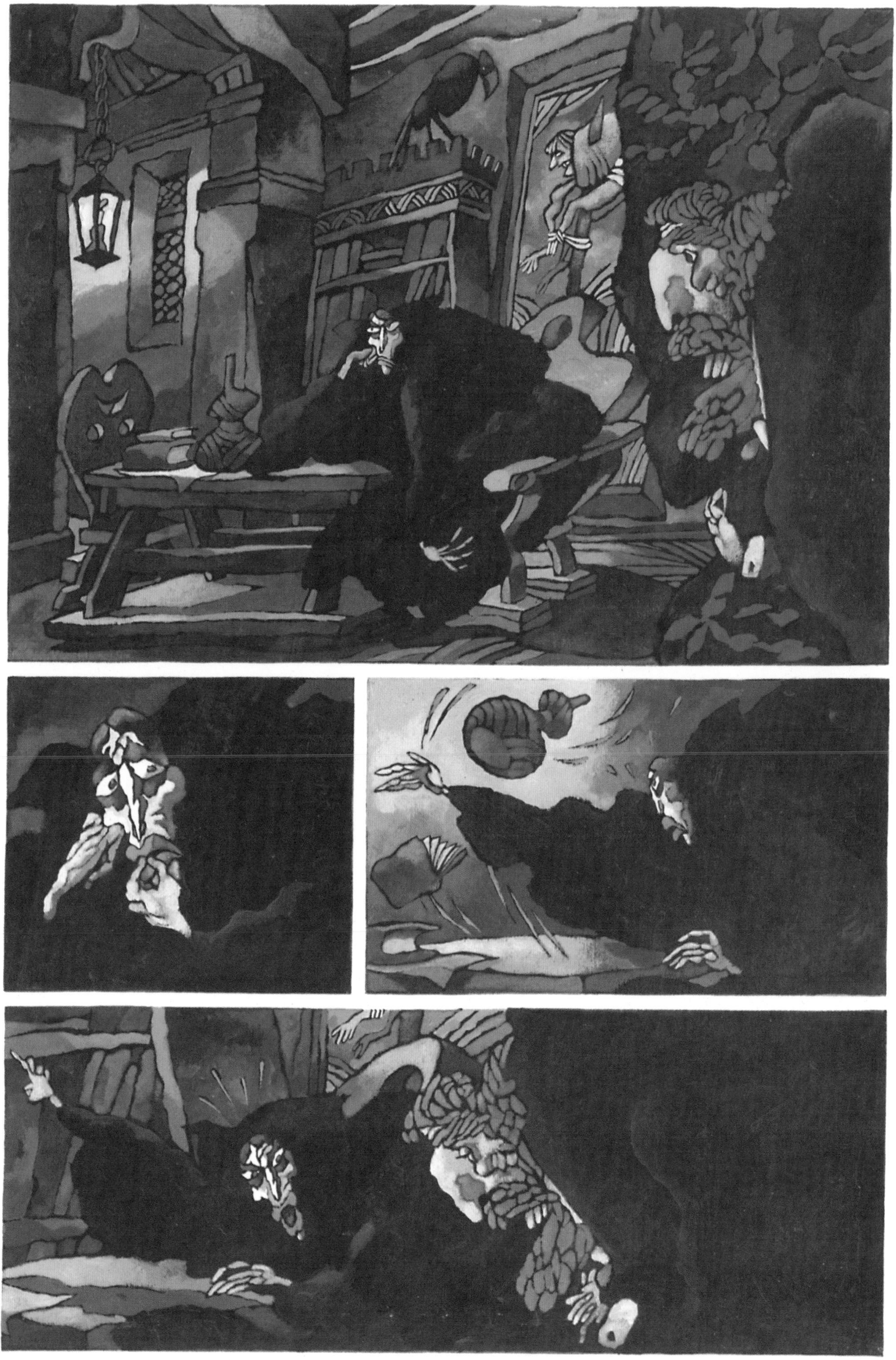

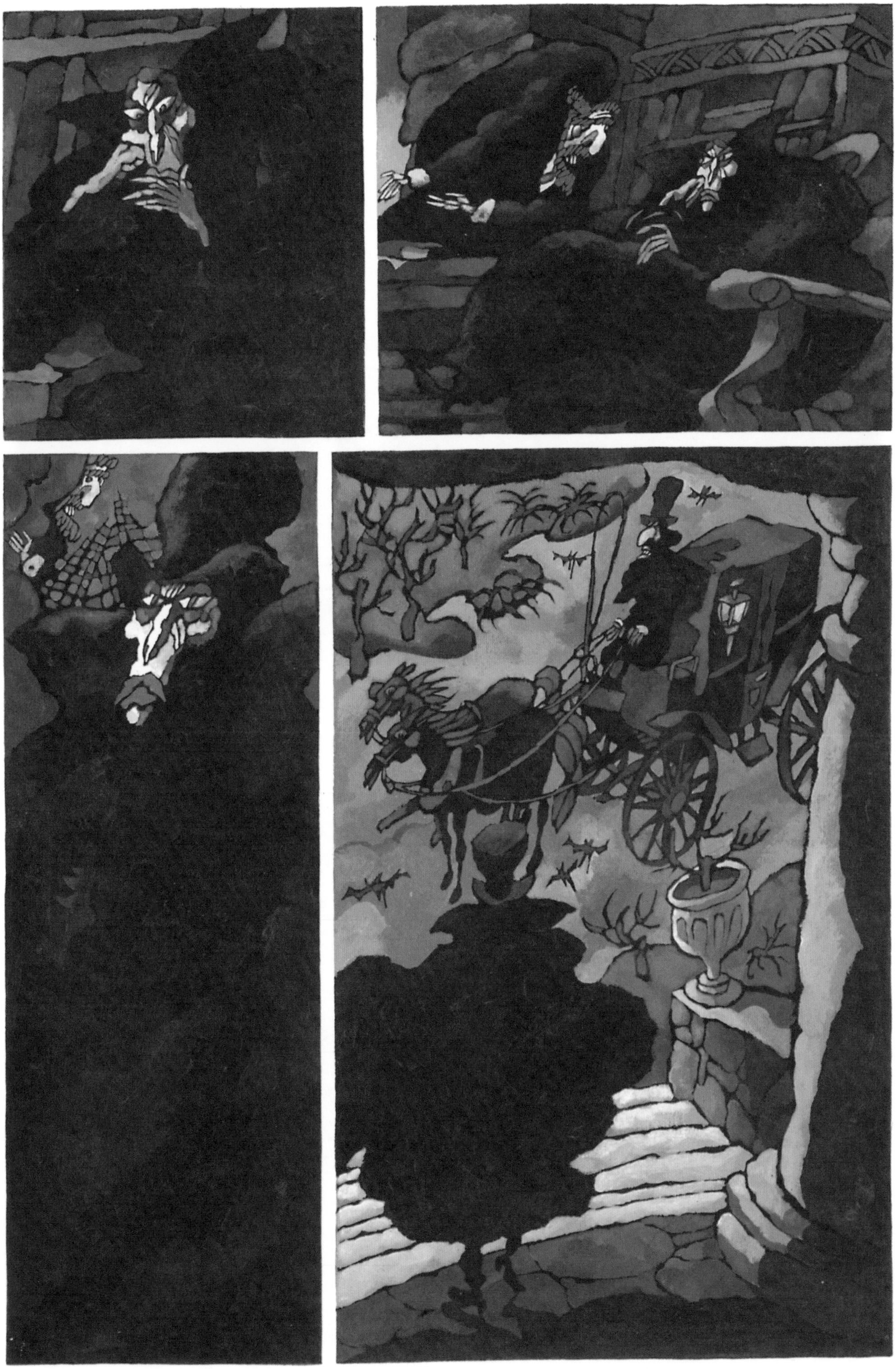

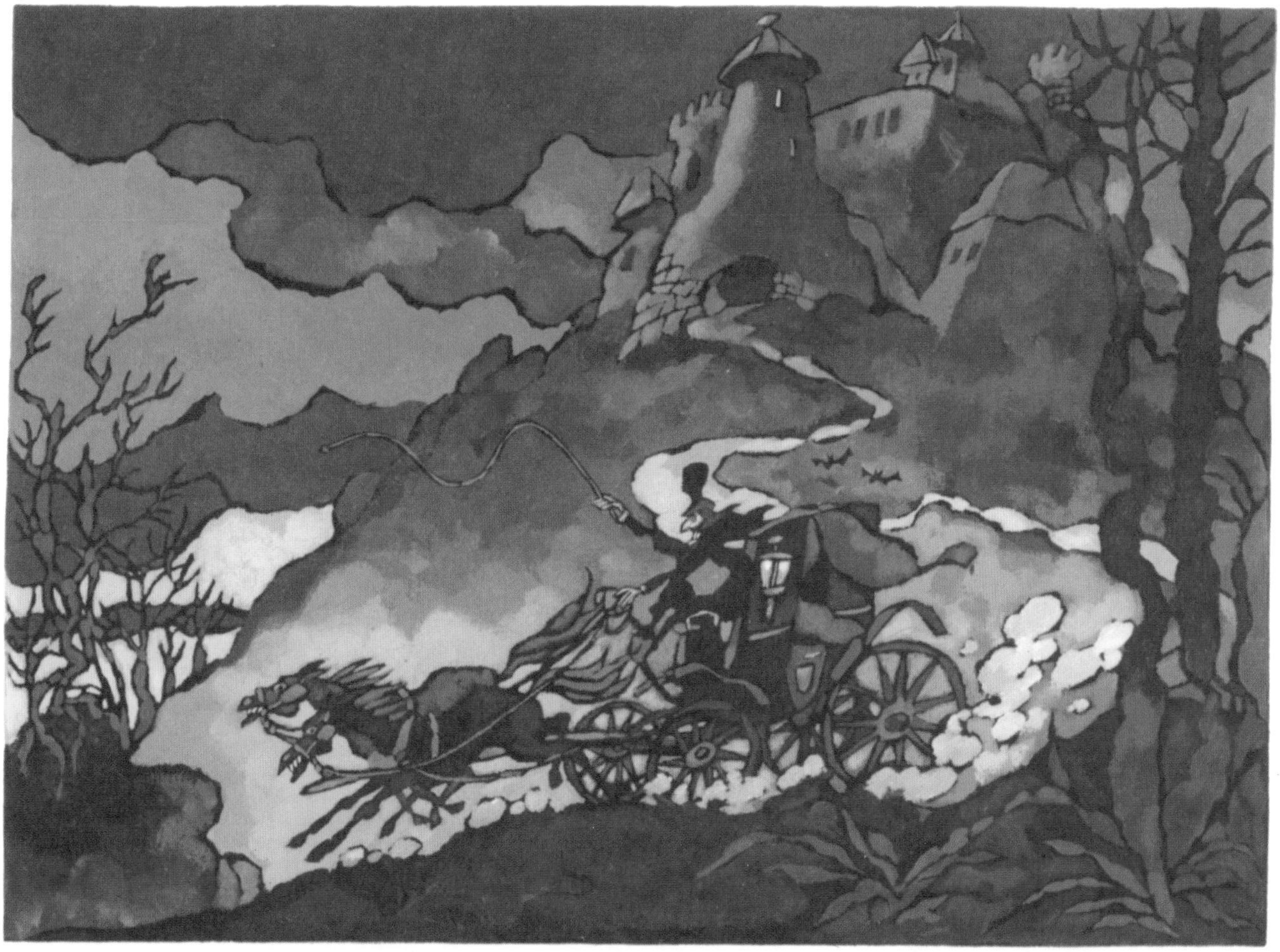

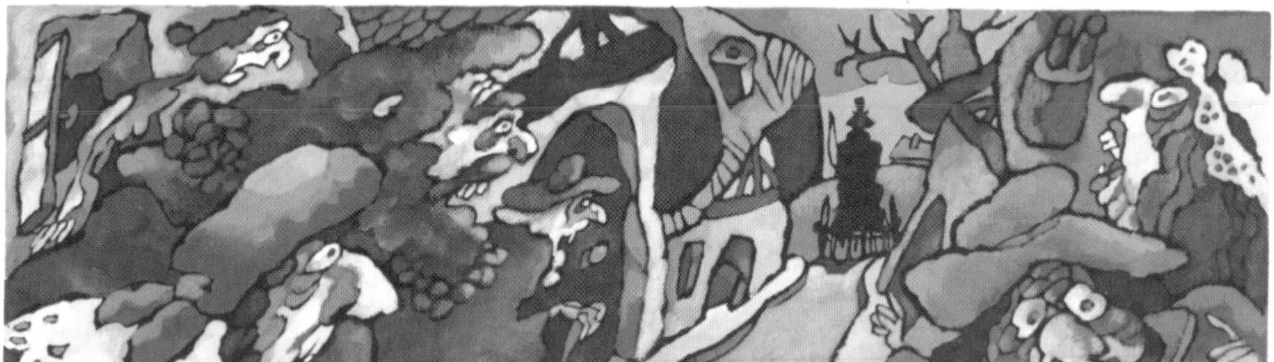

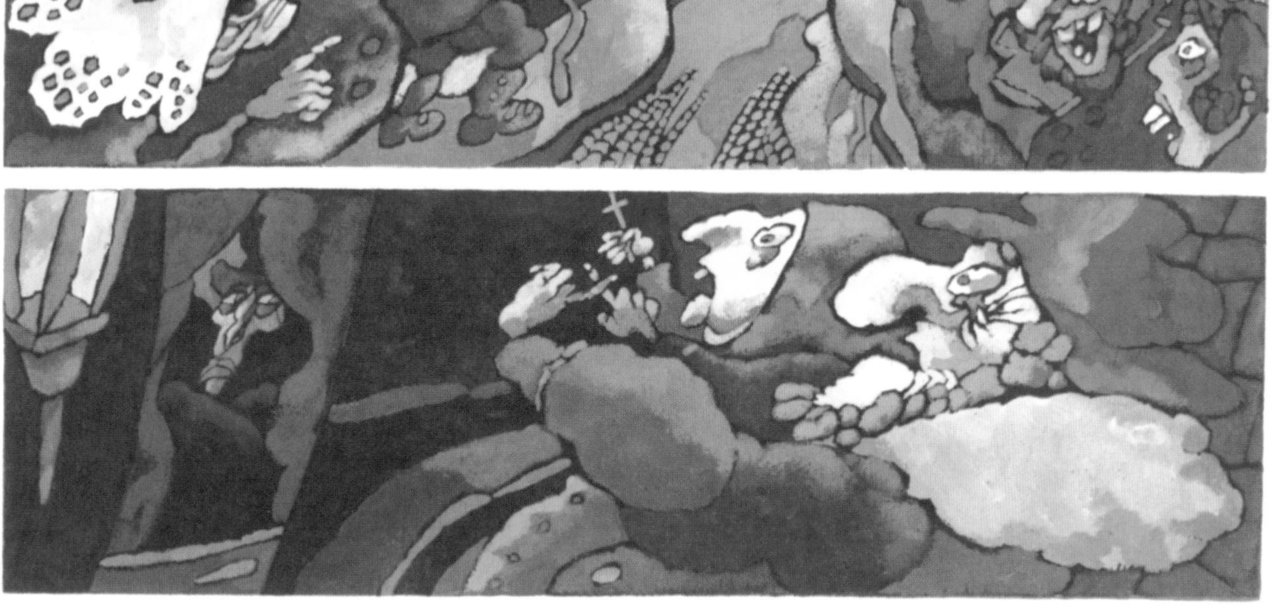

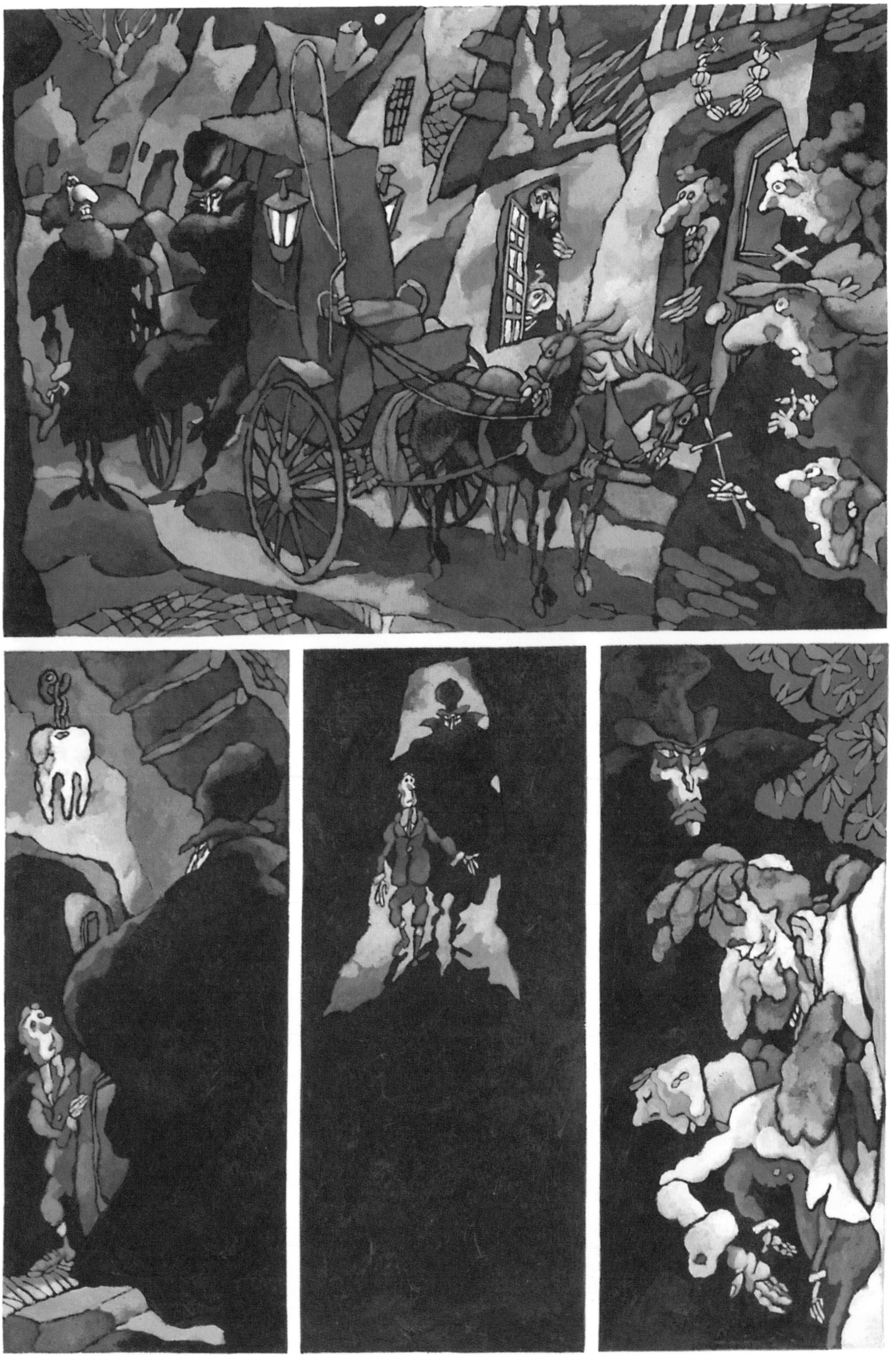

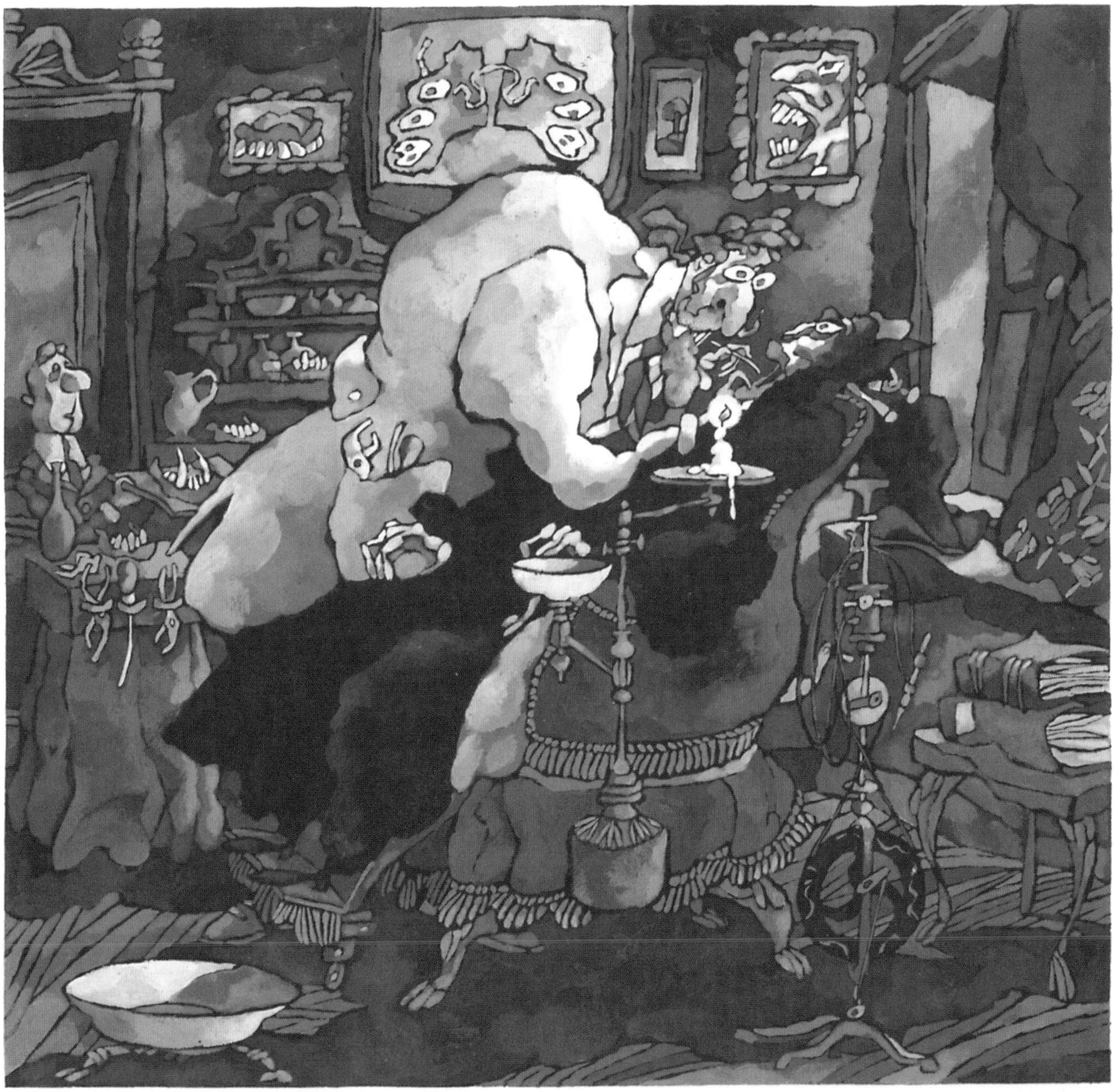

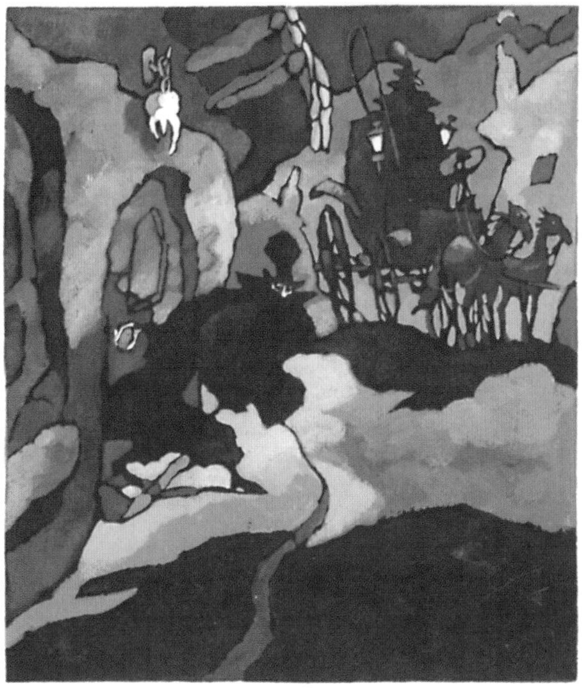

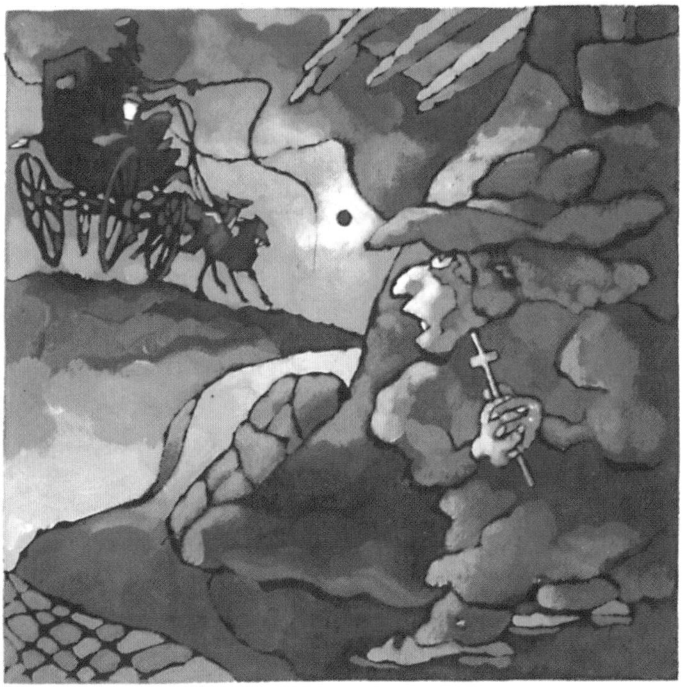

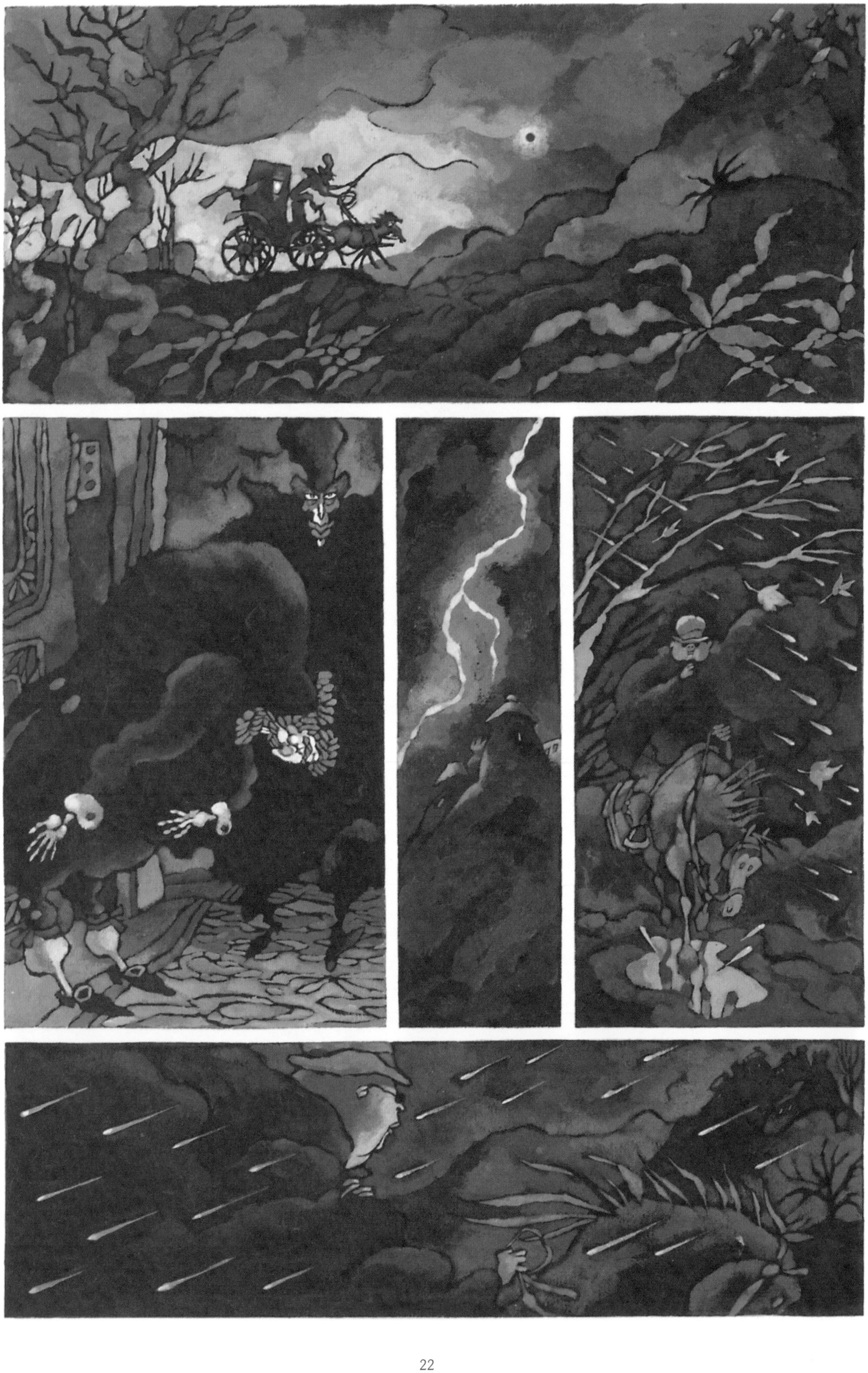

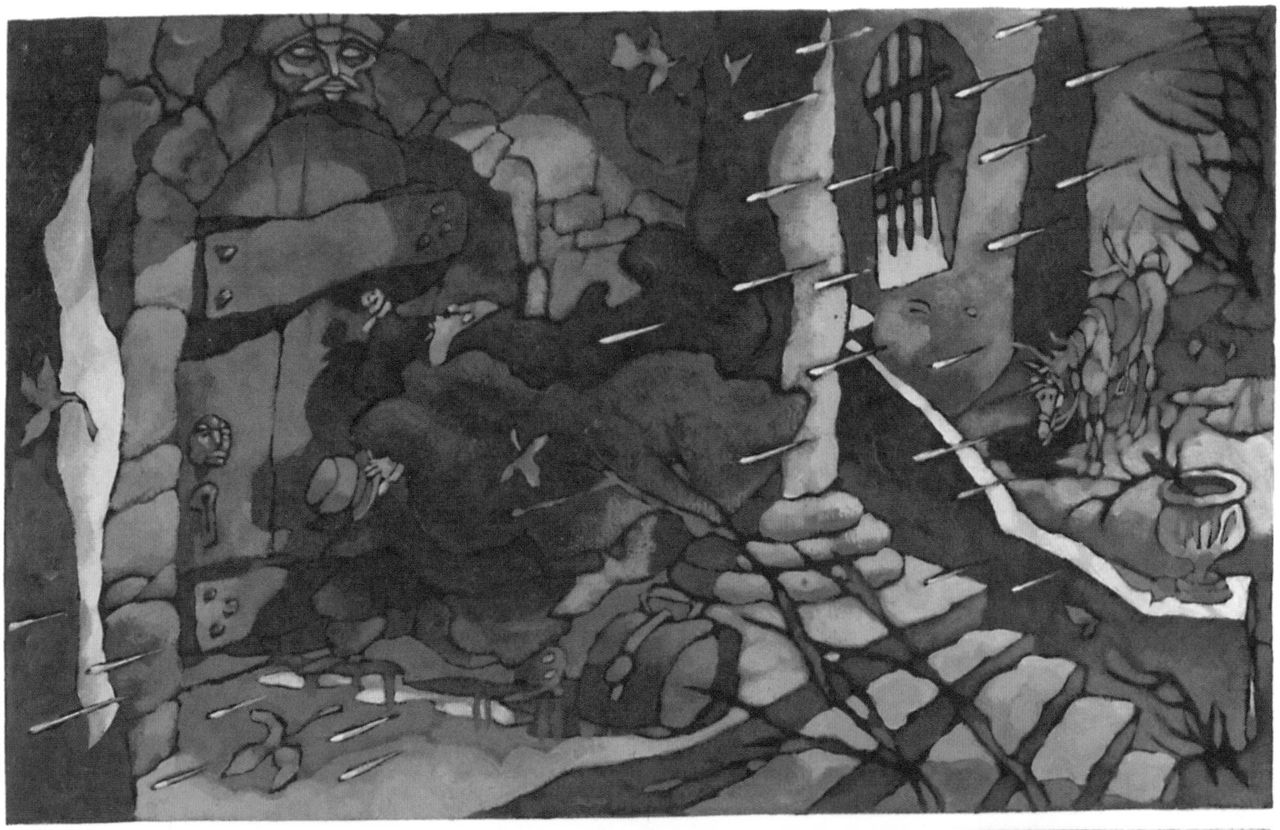

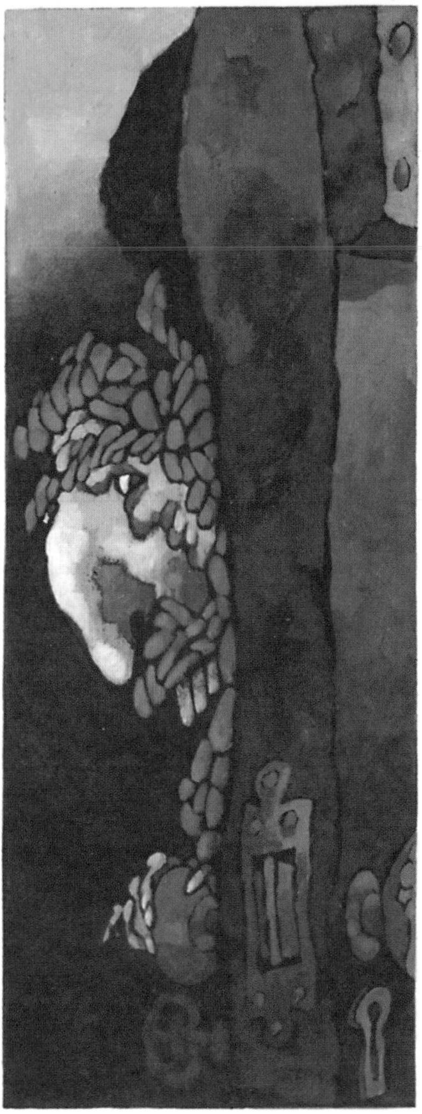

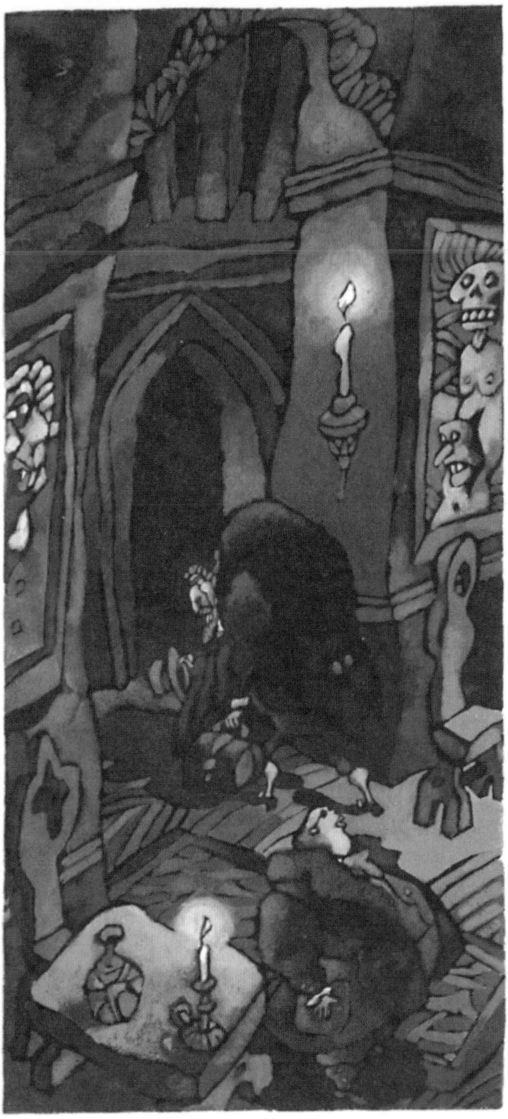

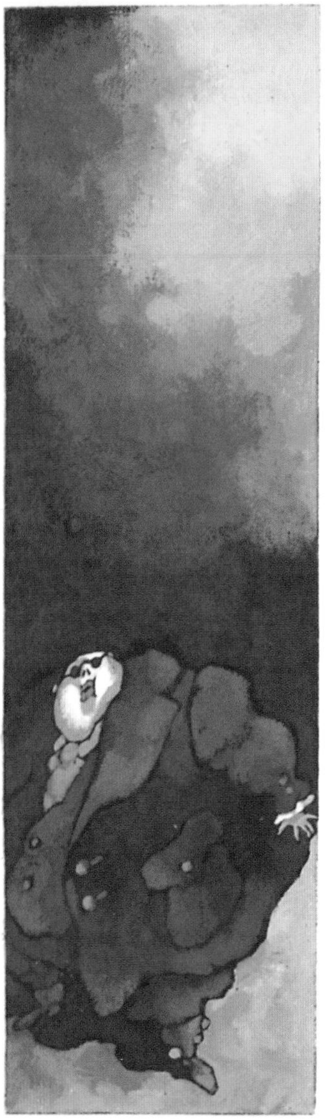

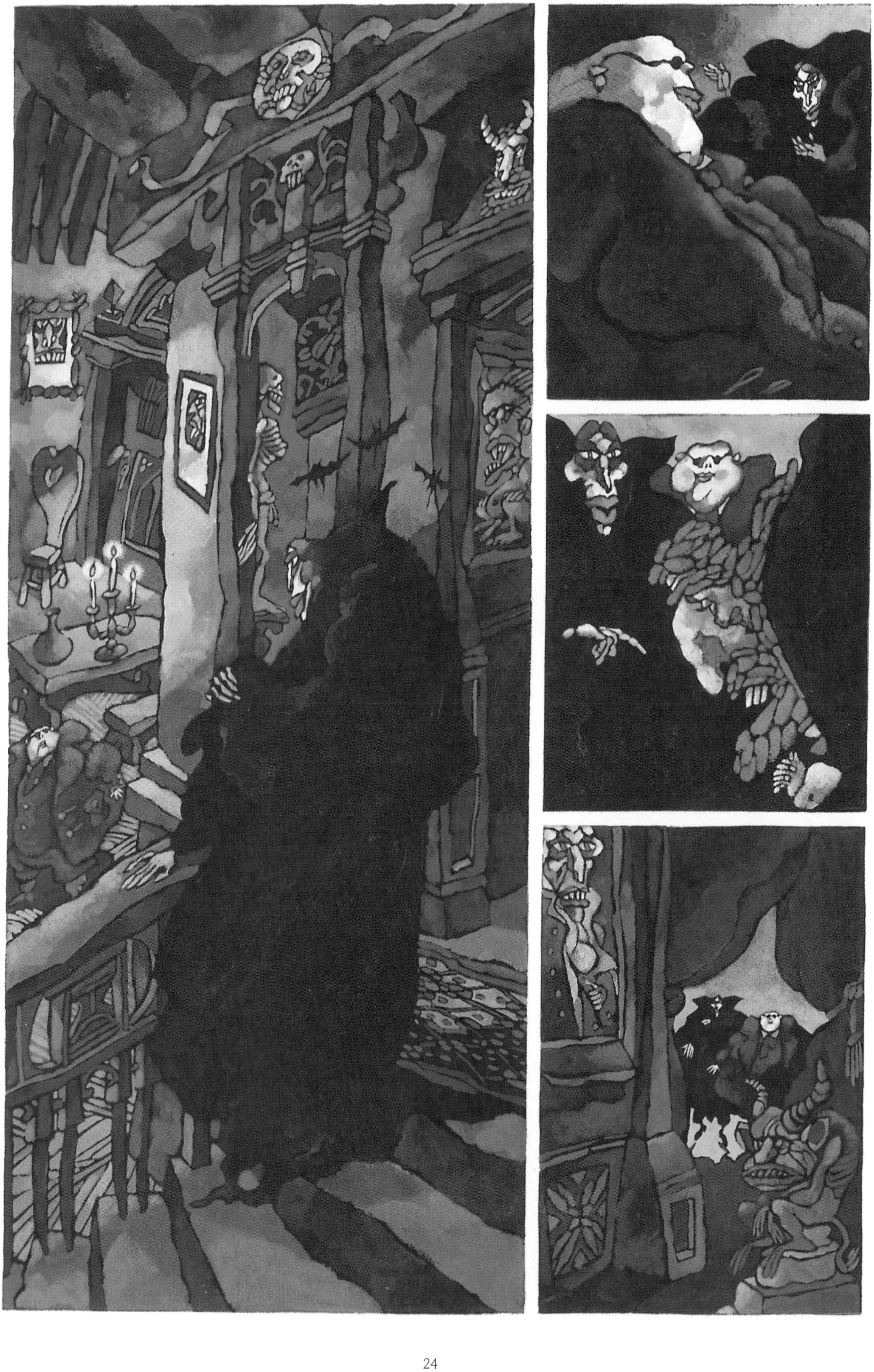

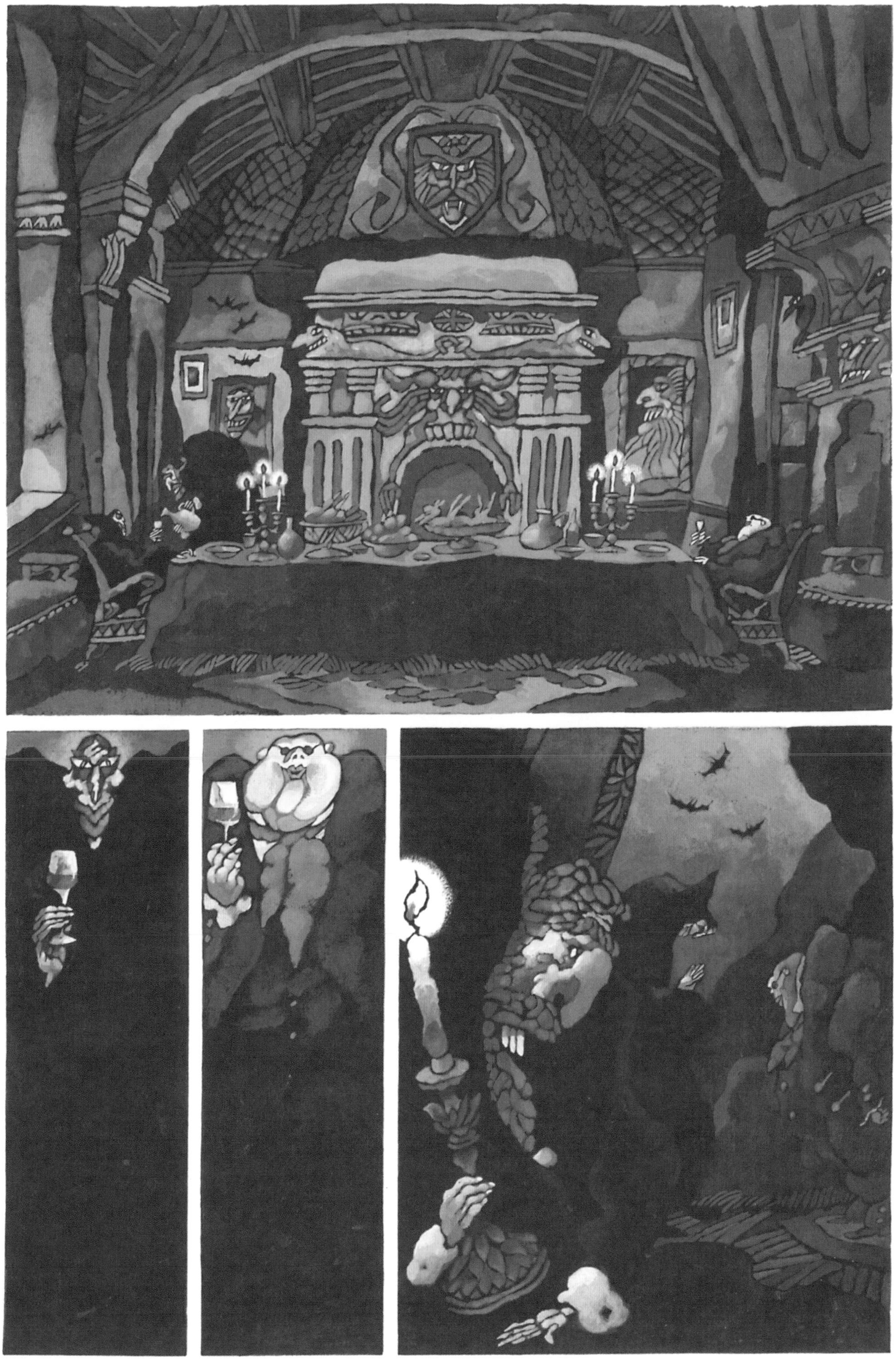

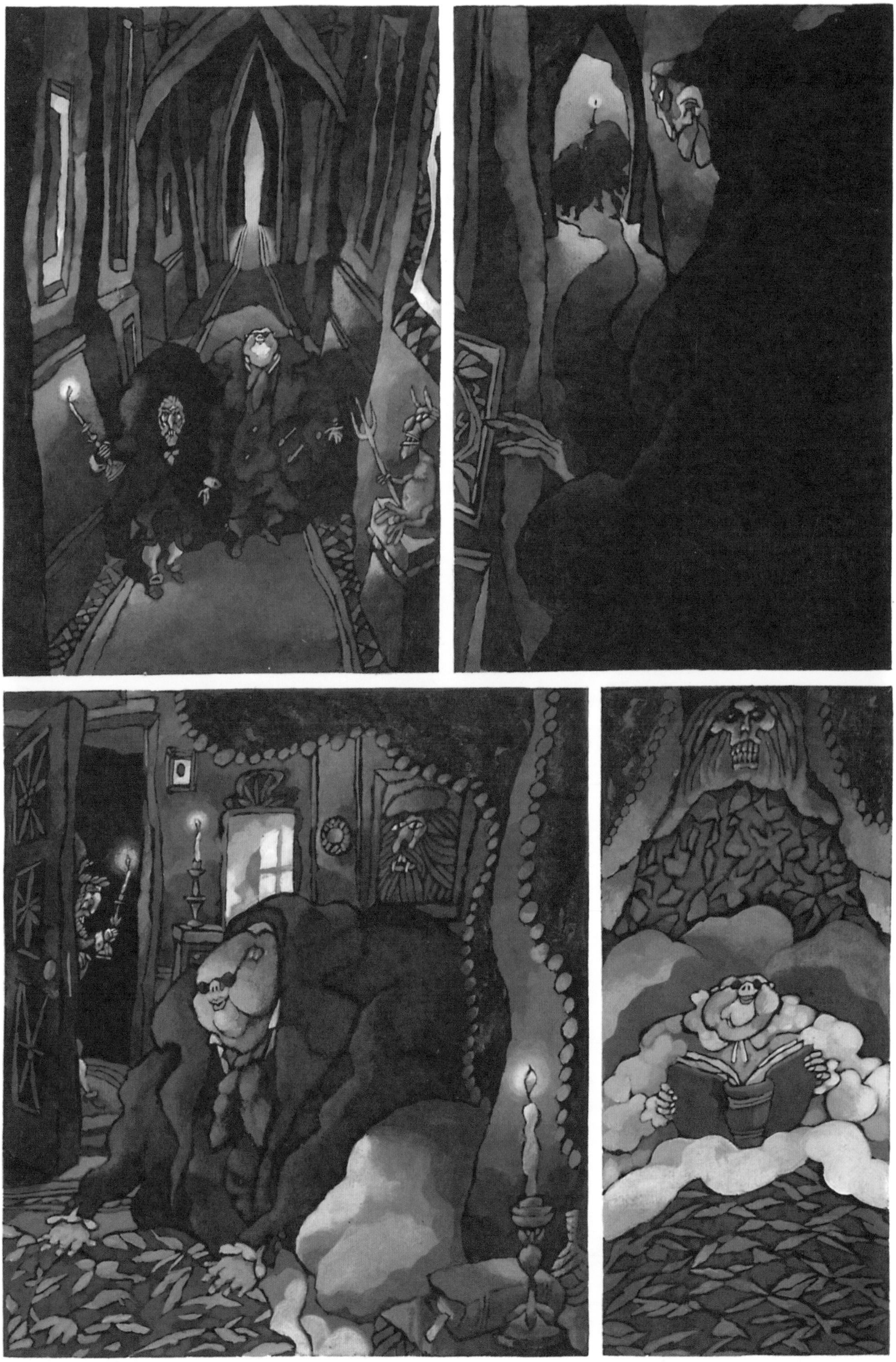

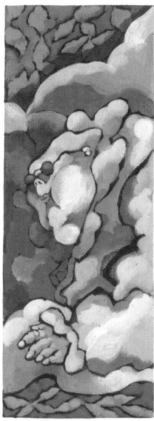
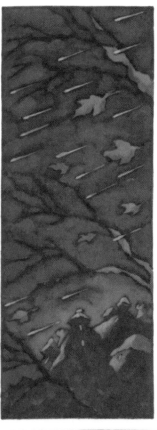

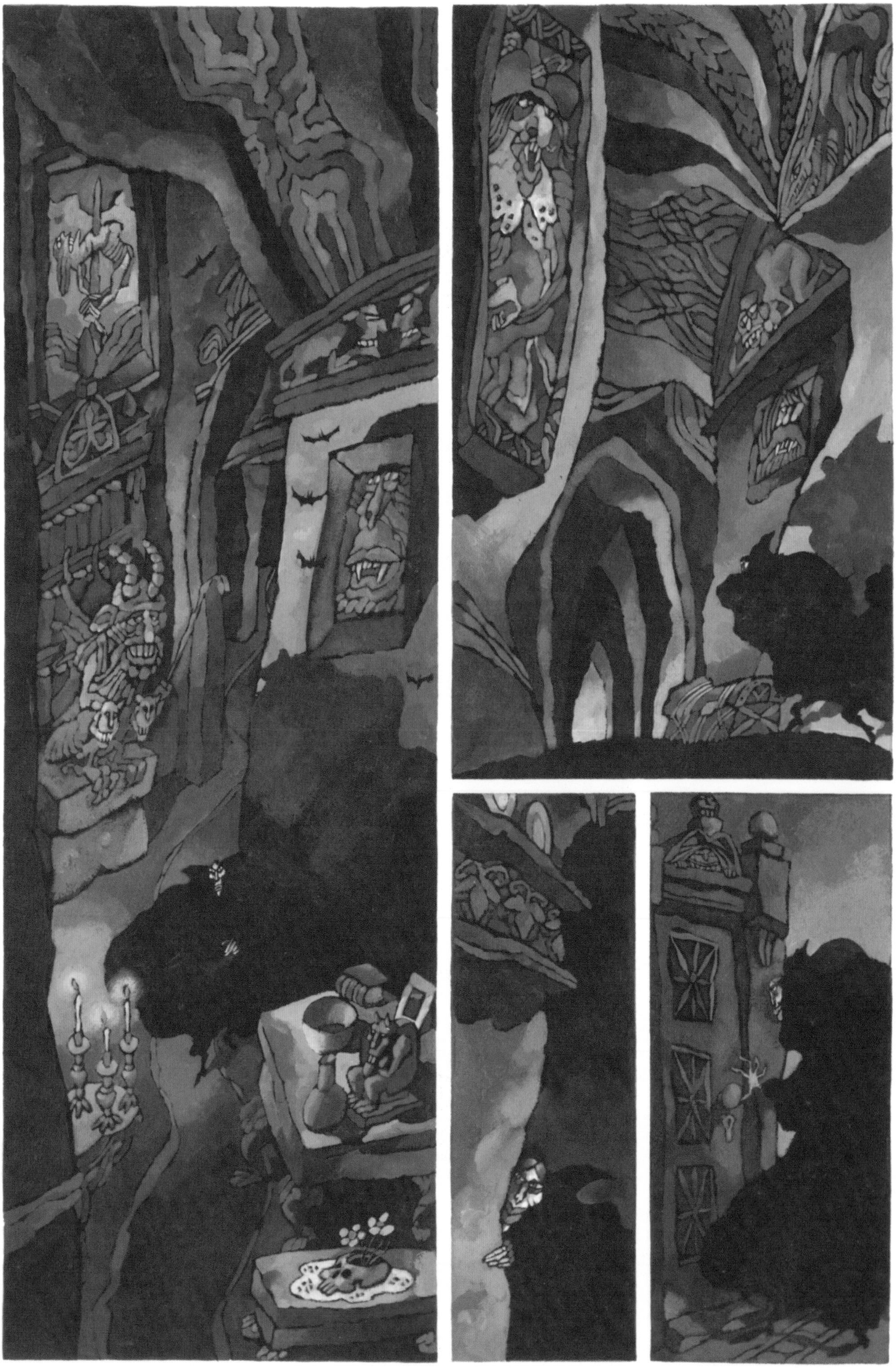

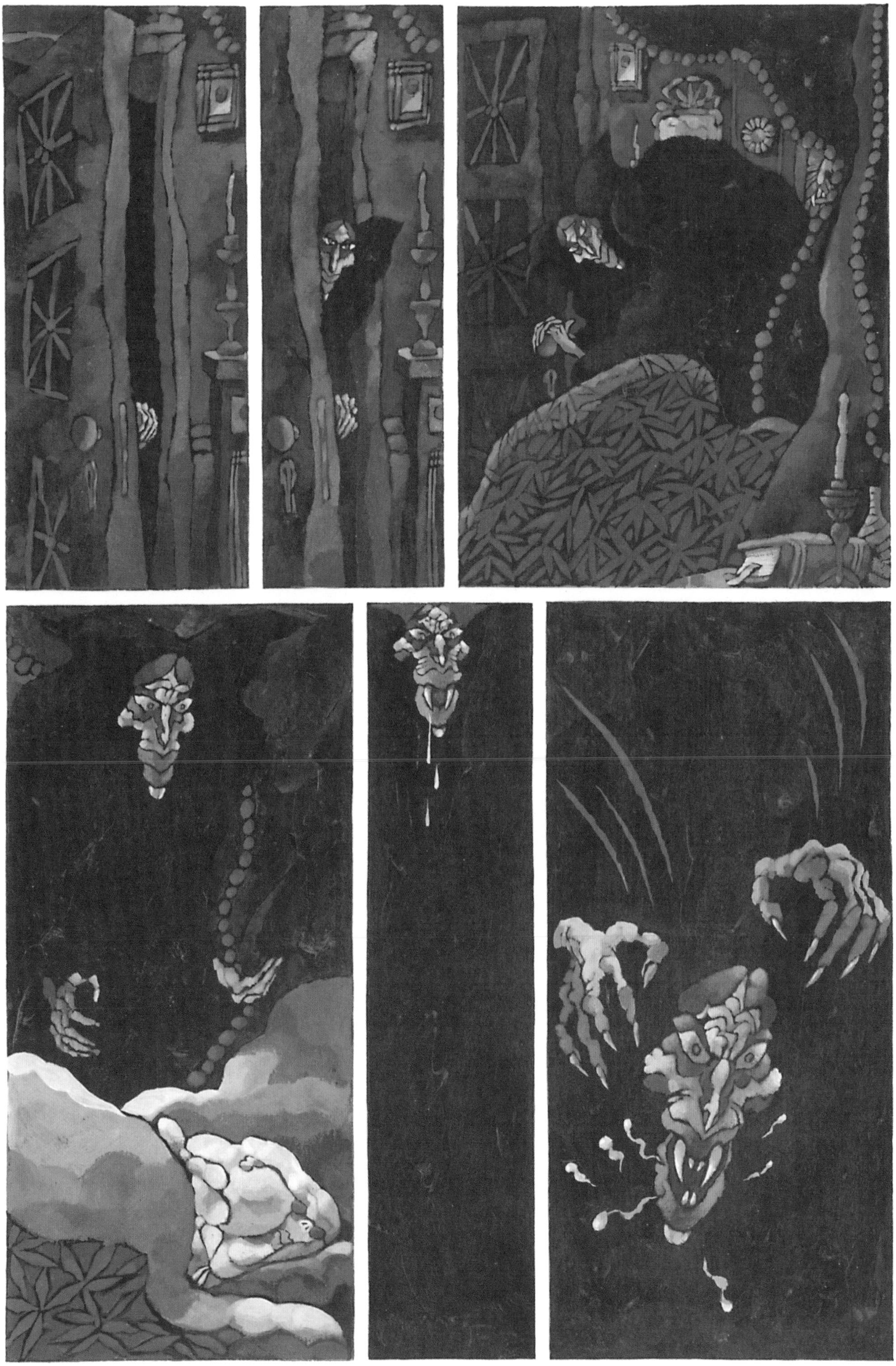

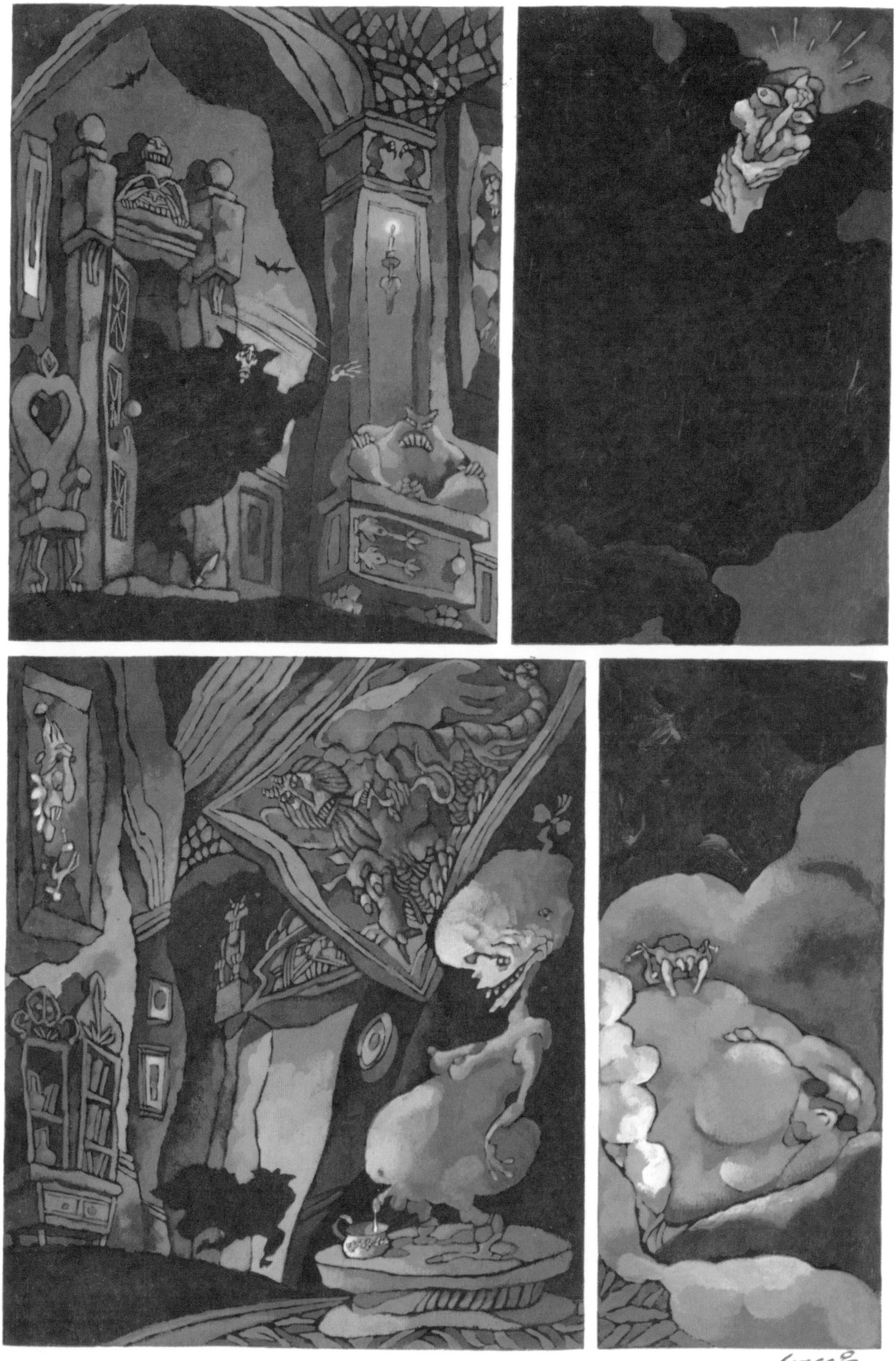

A Tender and Broken Heart

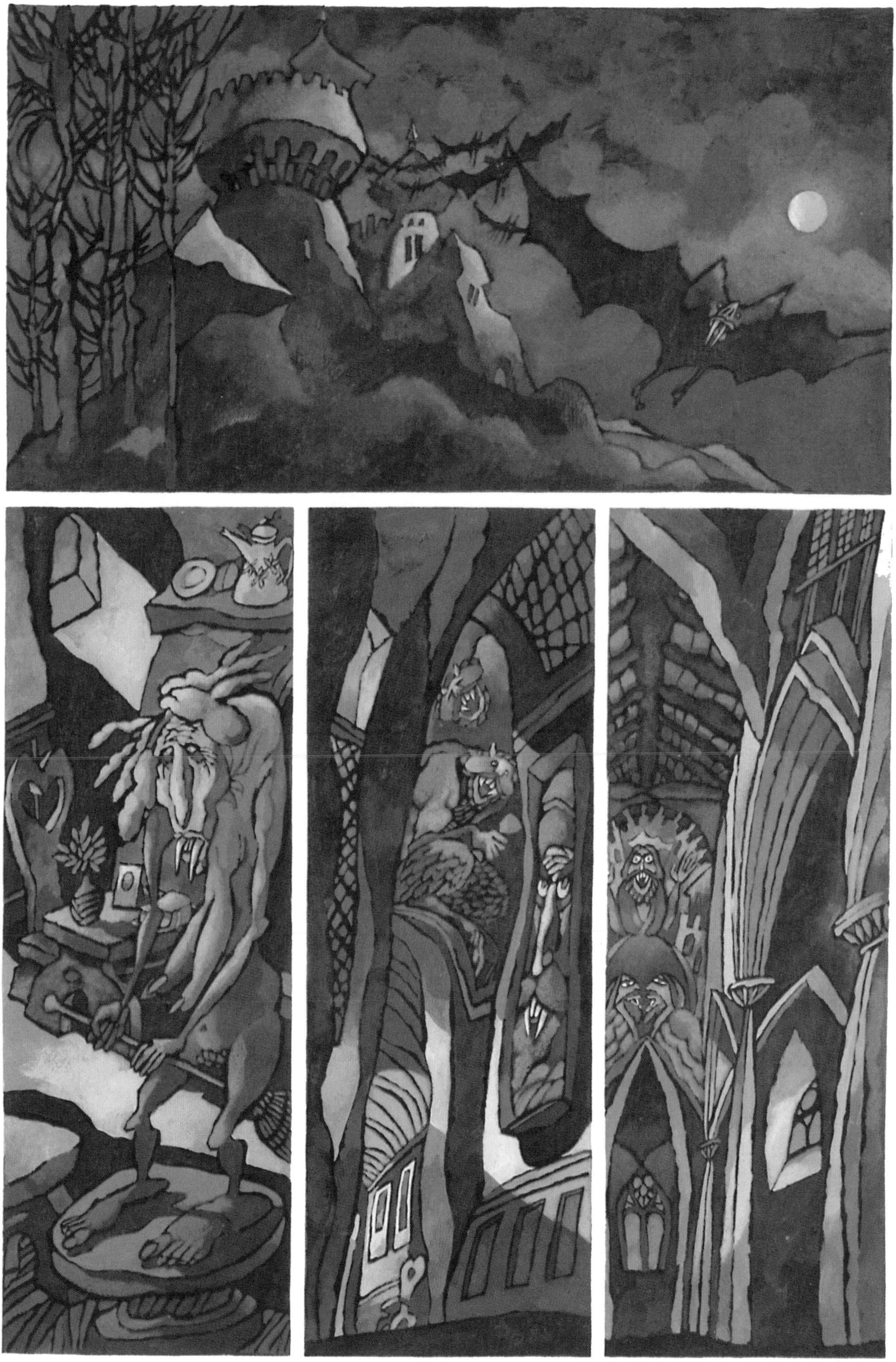

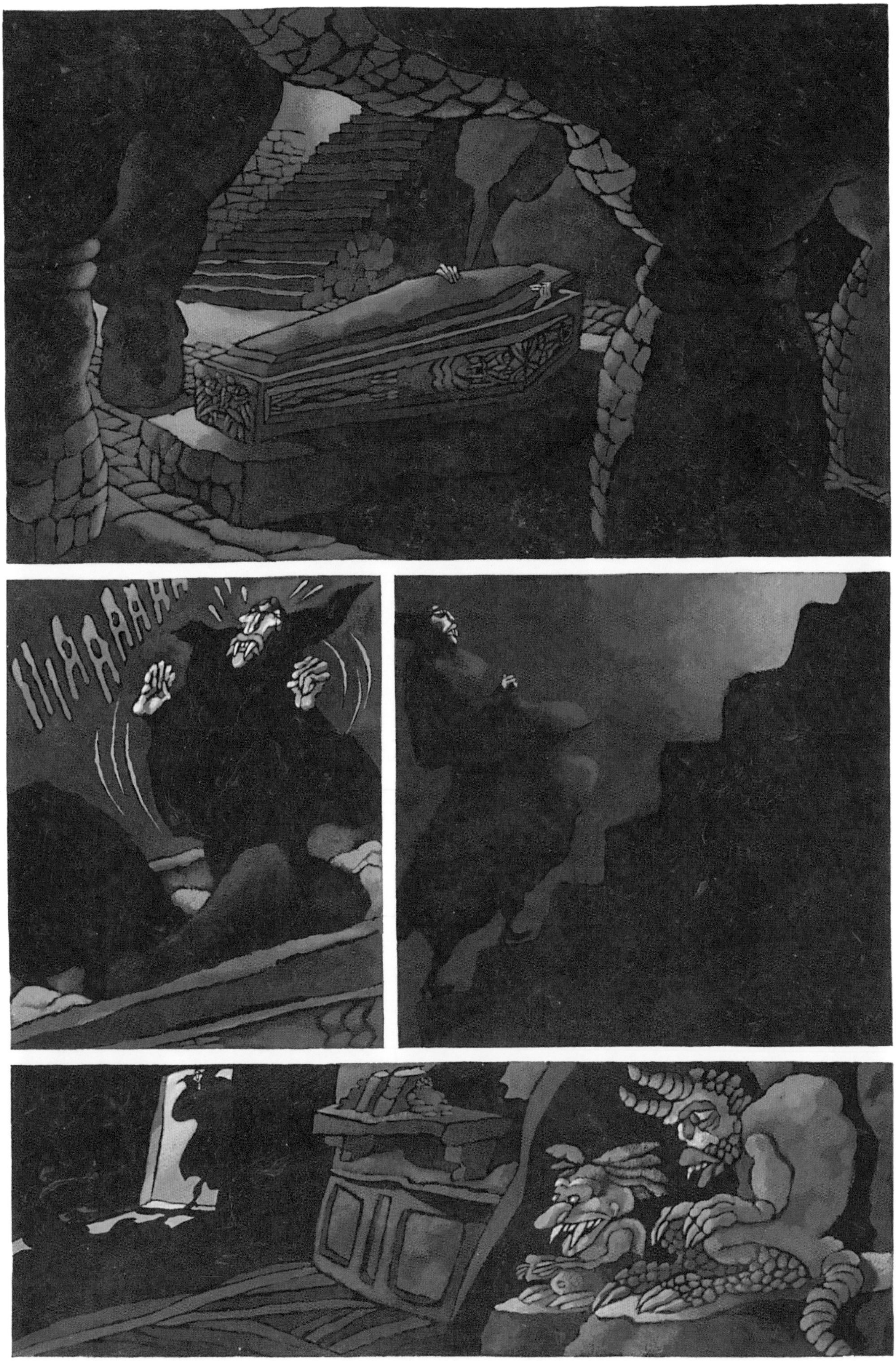

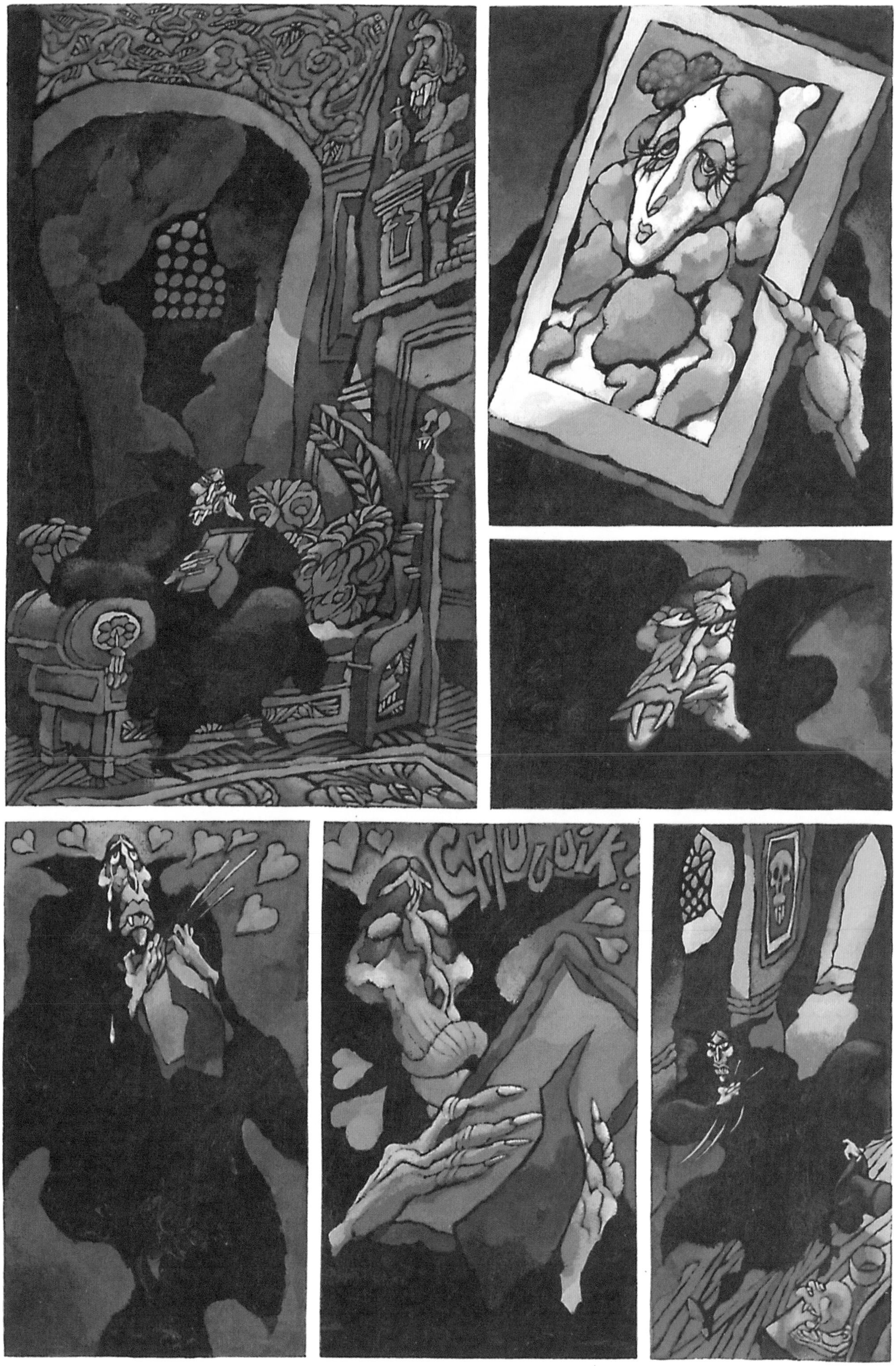
CHUUUIK!

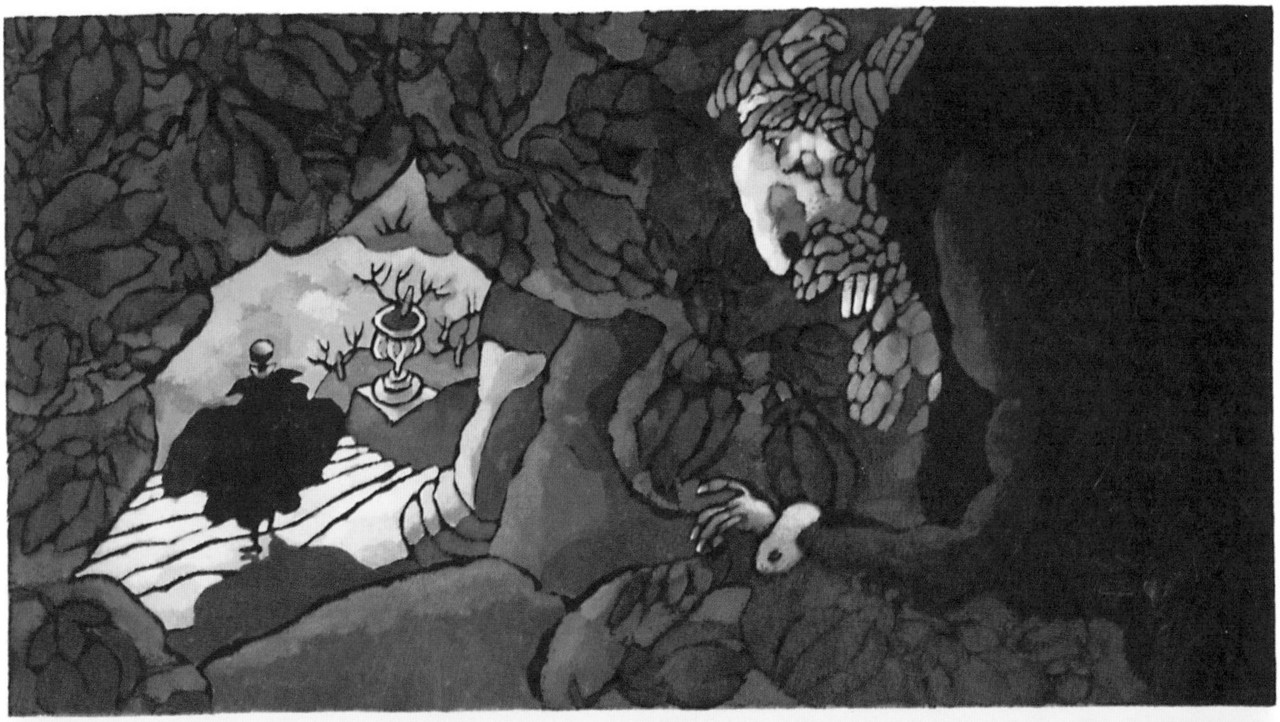

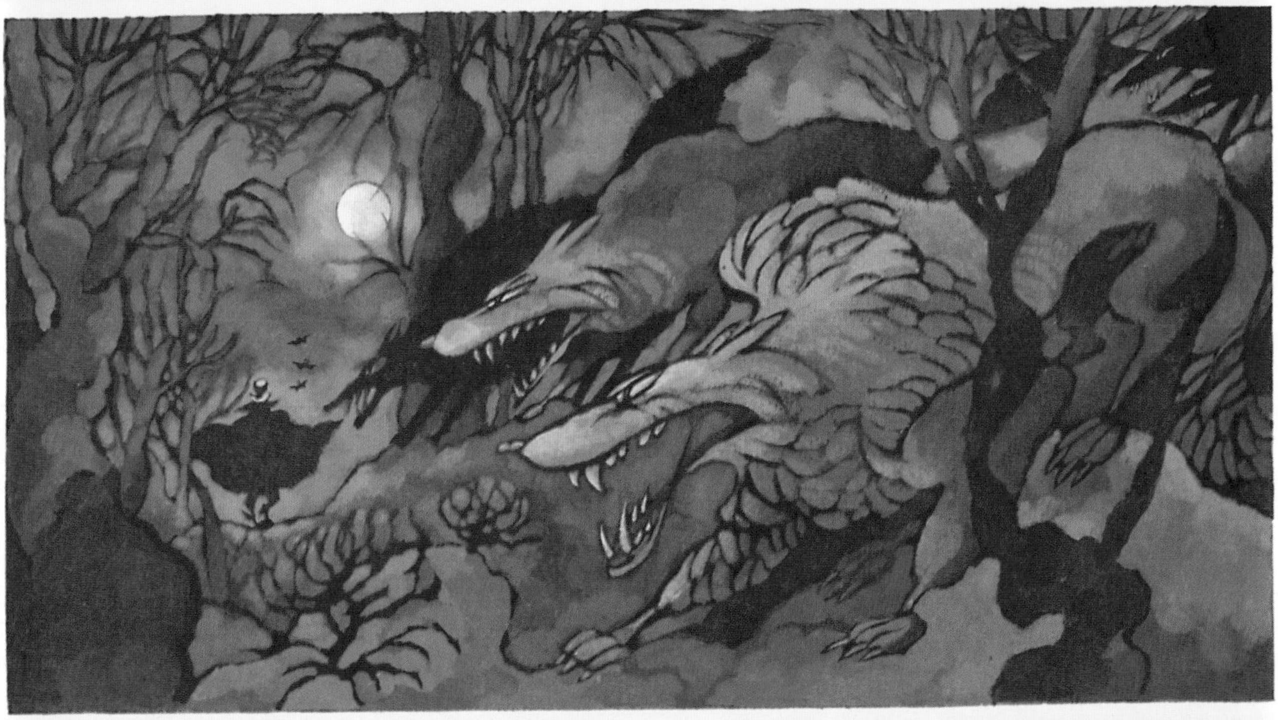

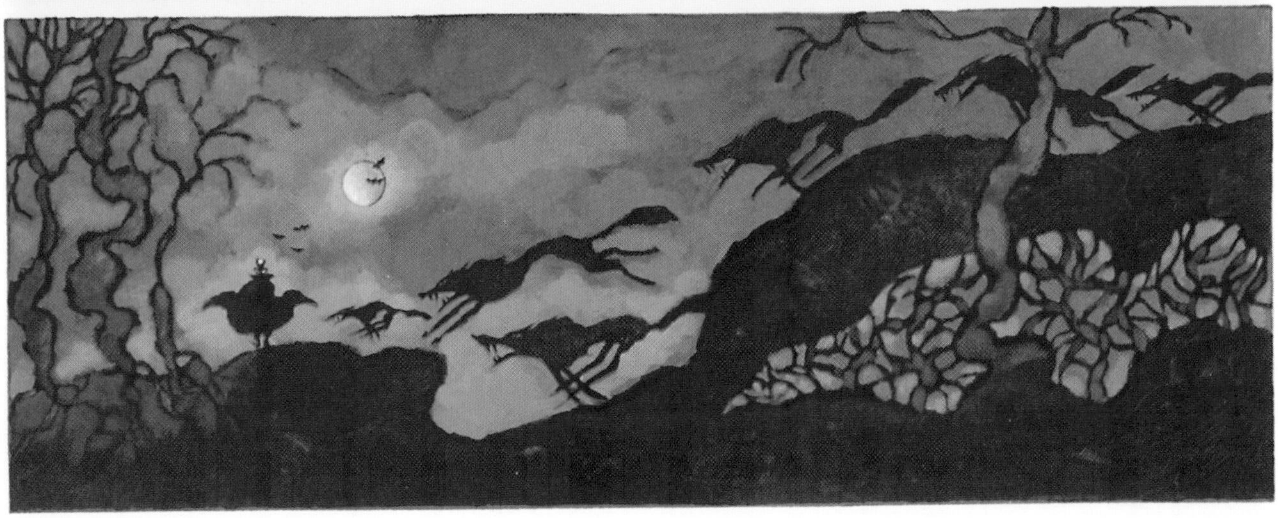

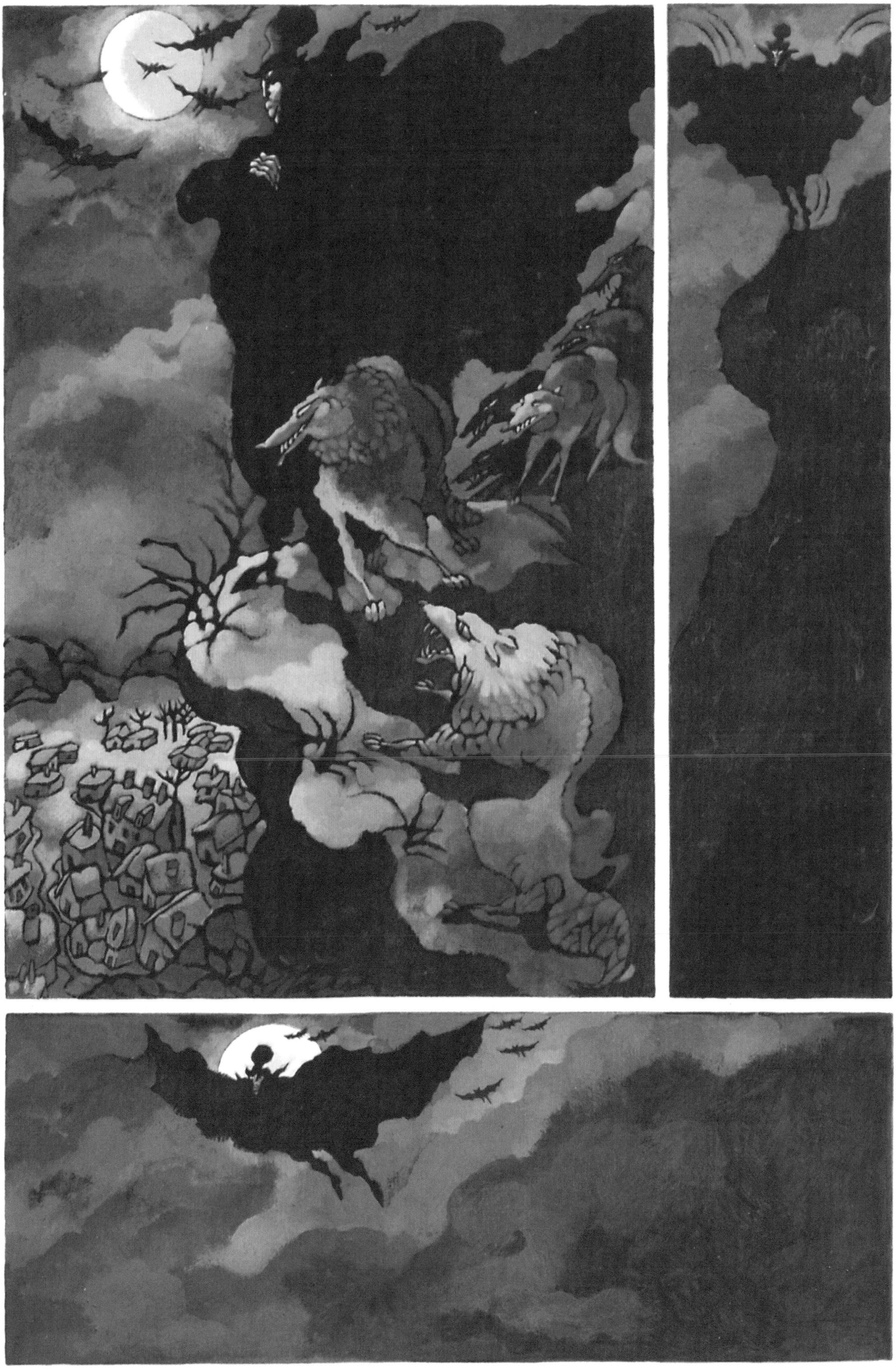

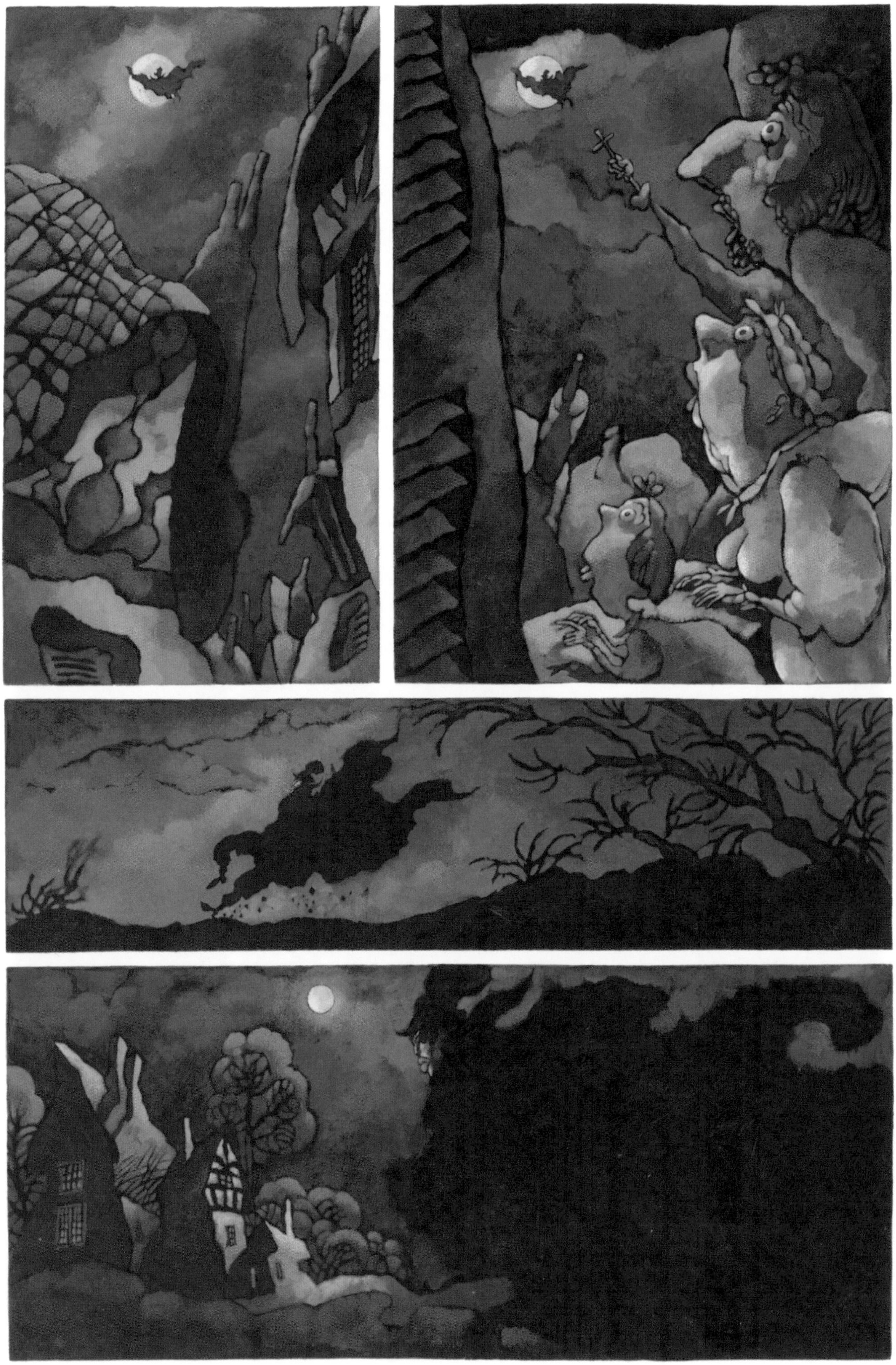

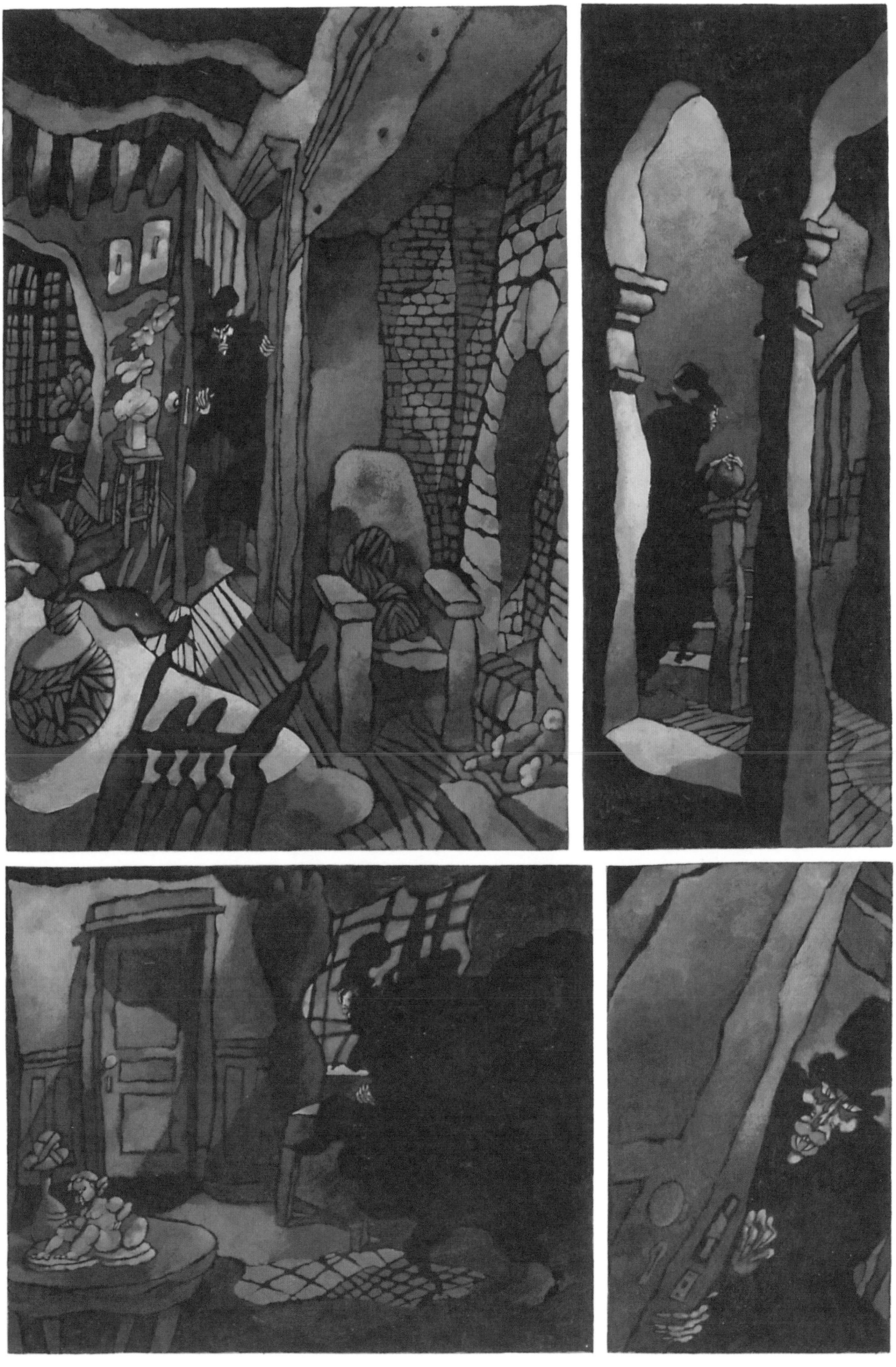

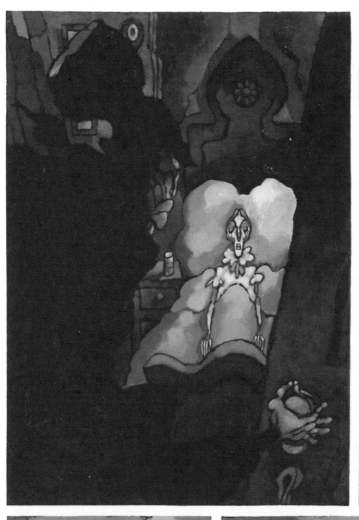

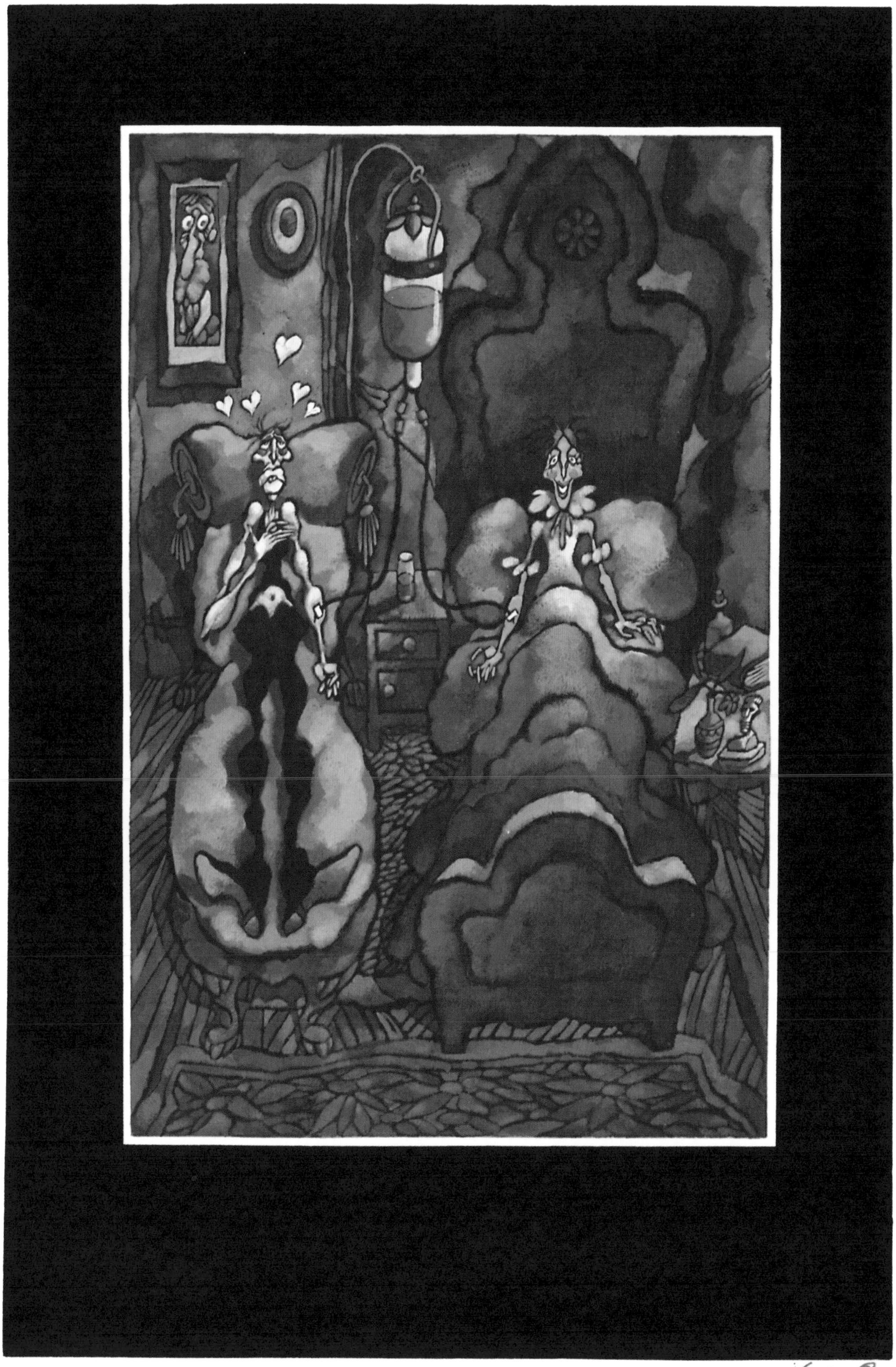

breccia

FOUR

I Was Legend

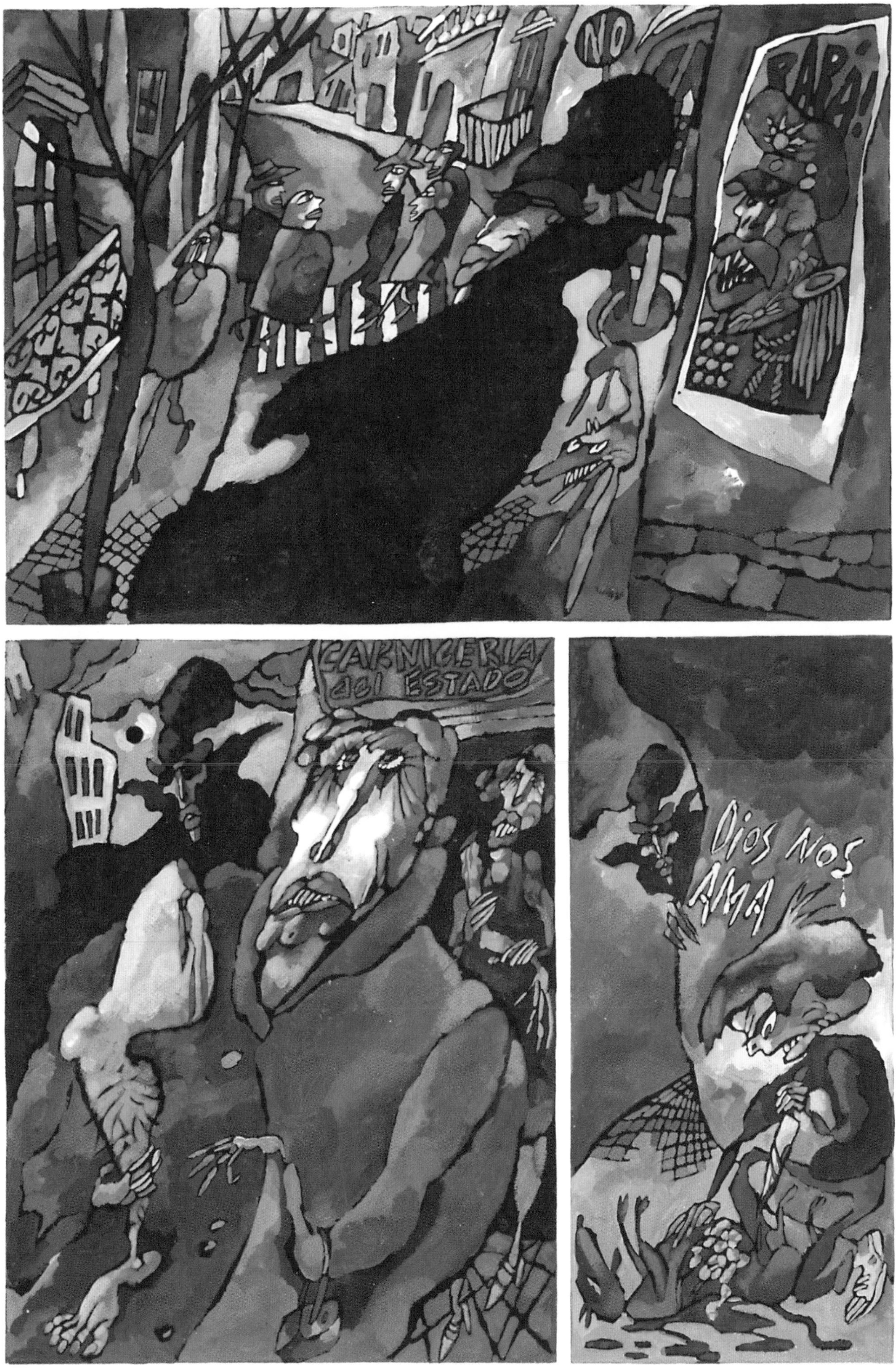
NO
PAPA!
CARNICERIA
del ESTADO
DIOS NOS
AMA

Carniceria del Estado: State Butcher Shop *Dios Nos Ama*: God Loves Us

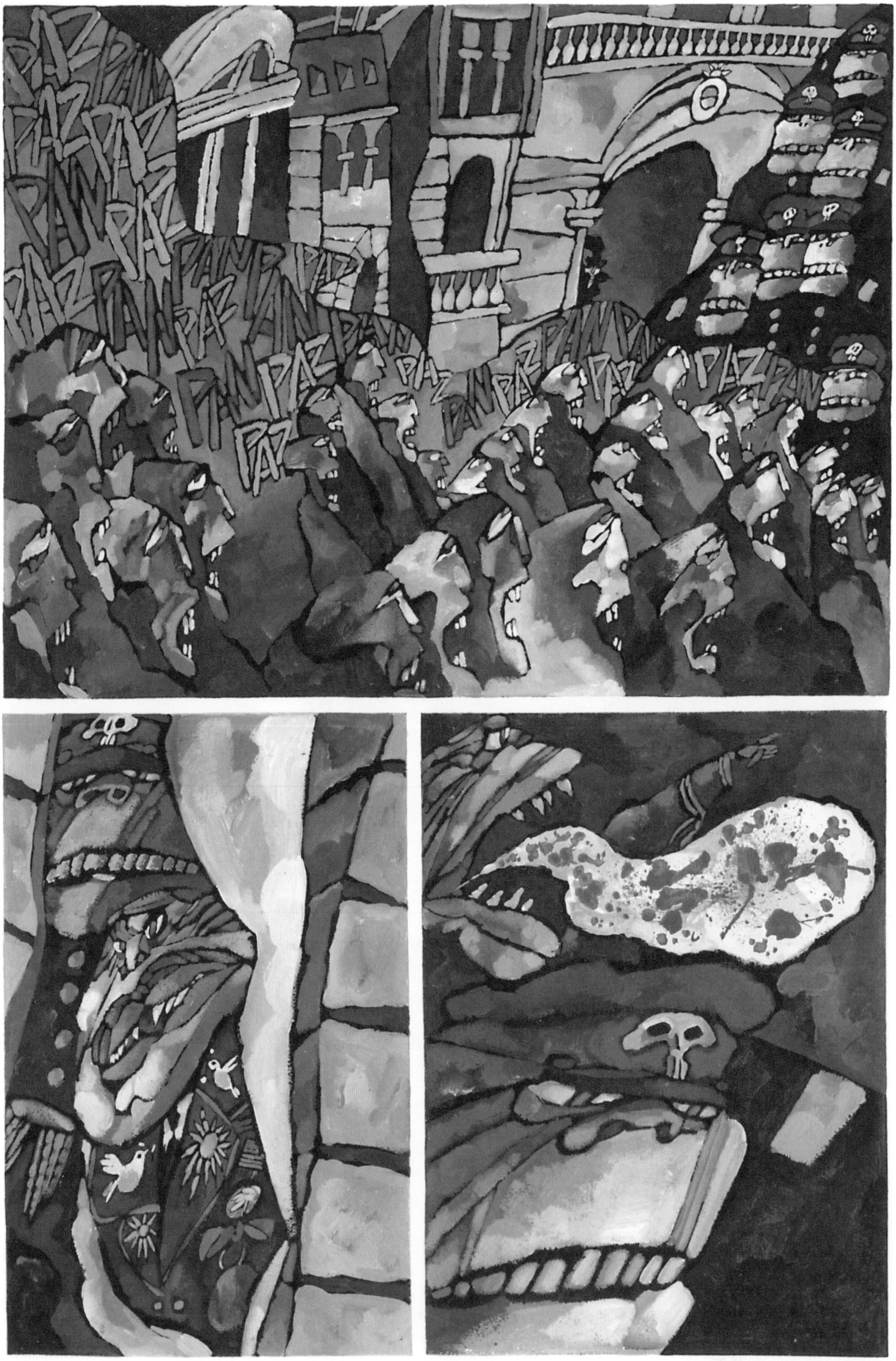
PAZ
PAN

Paz: Peace

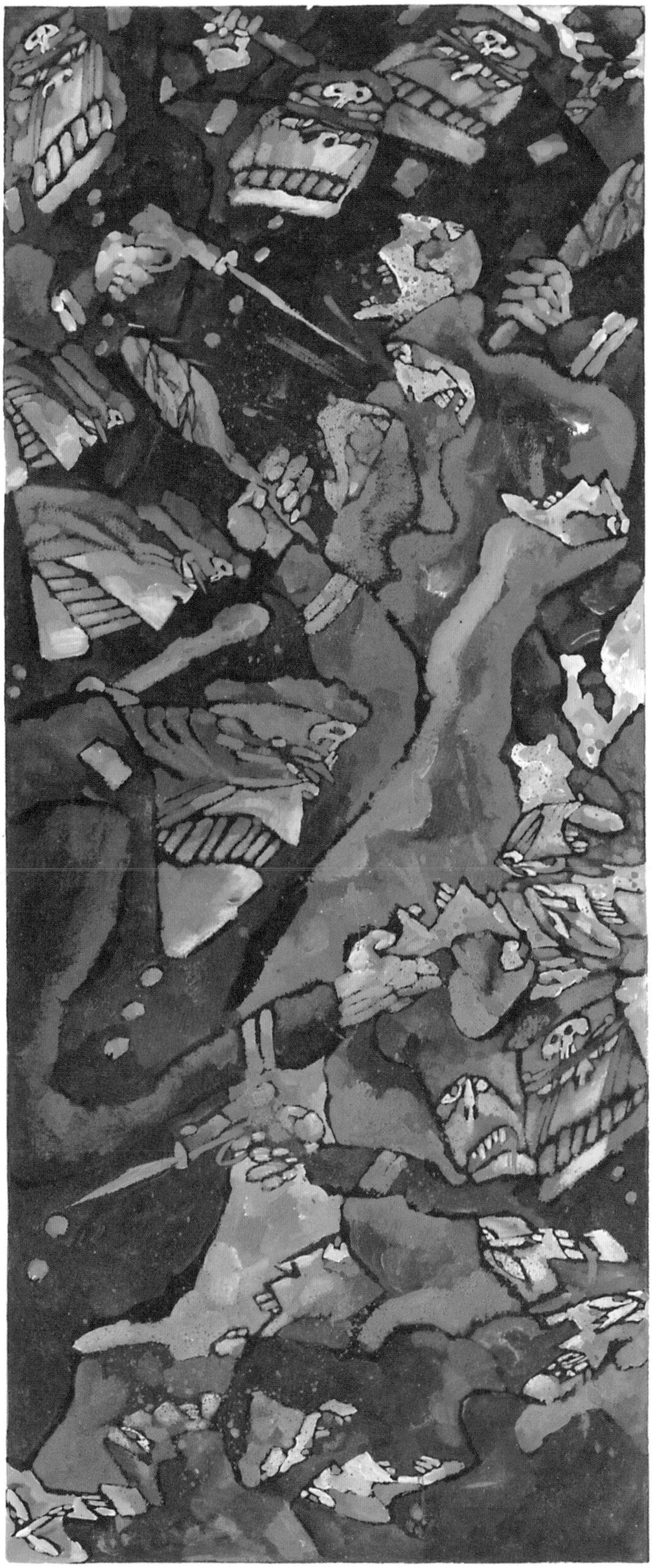

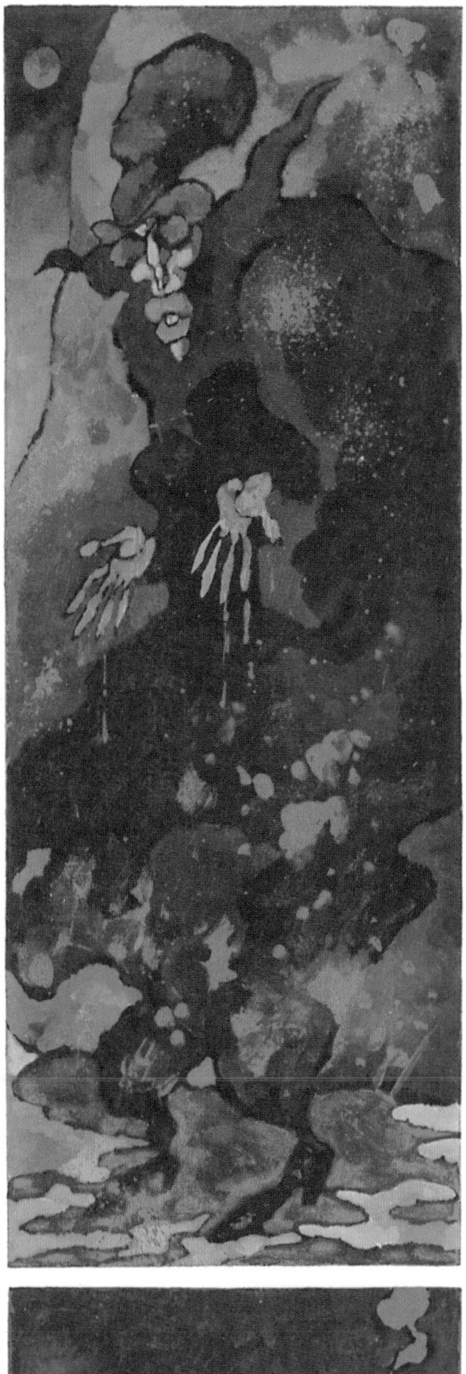

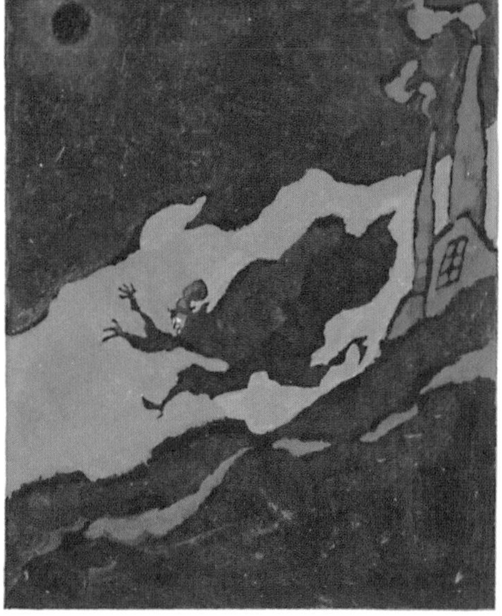

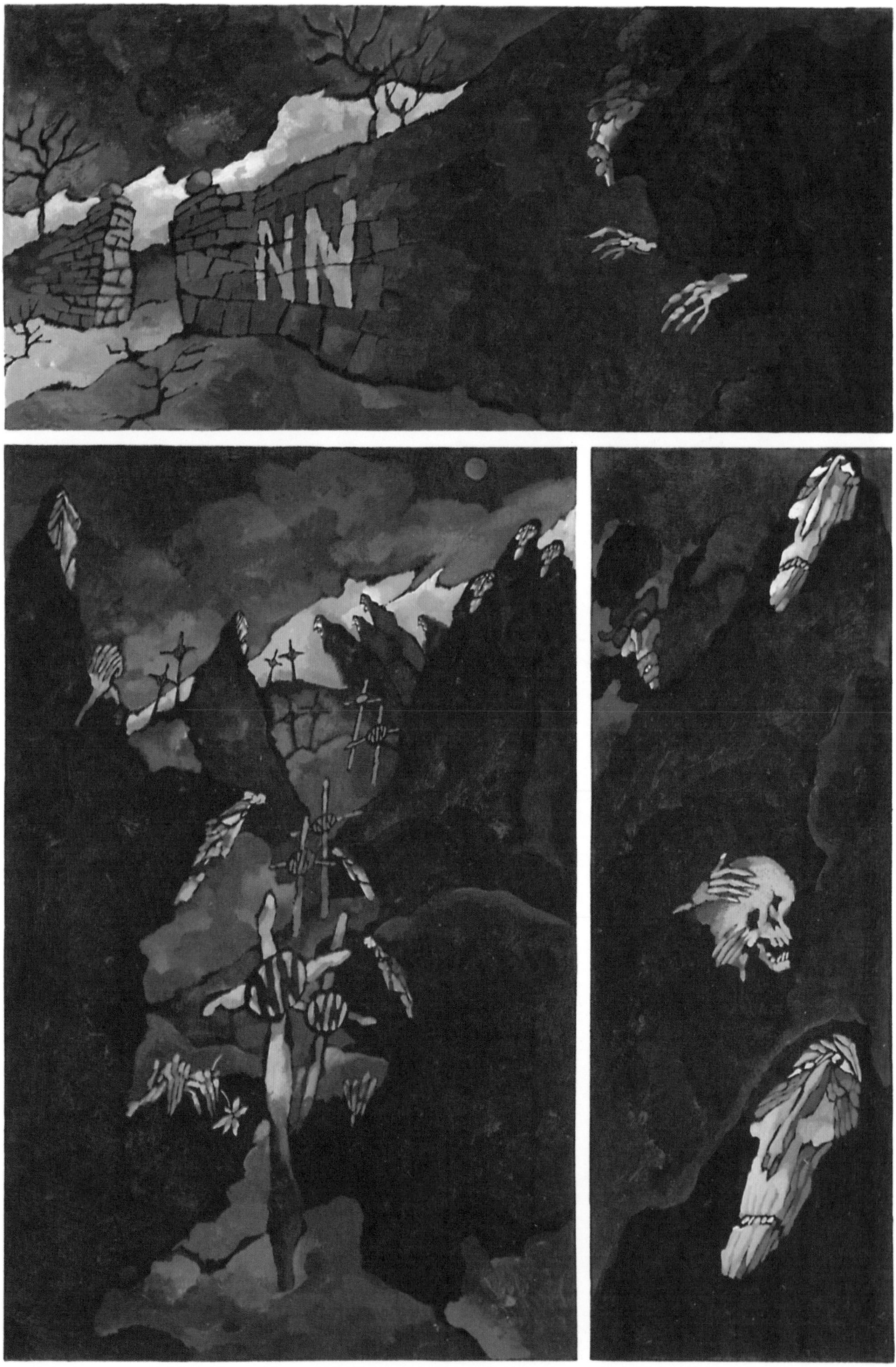
NN

NN ningún nombre, "the nameless": NN marks mass graves of unidentified people. Many of the "disappeared" were young, and in some countries, bodies would be "adopted" and mourned.

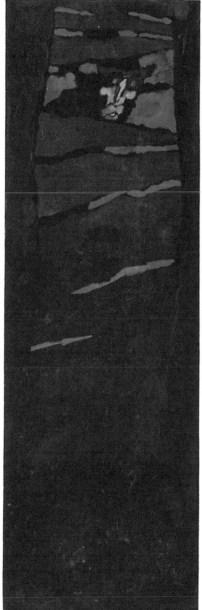

desperdicios: waste
Boleta 1038: Boleta can mean ballot and/or ticket (as in bill for payment) in Argentina.
Colloquially, there's also a phrase that's the equivalent of you're number/ticket is up, i.e., you're dead.

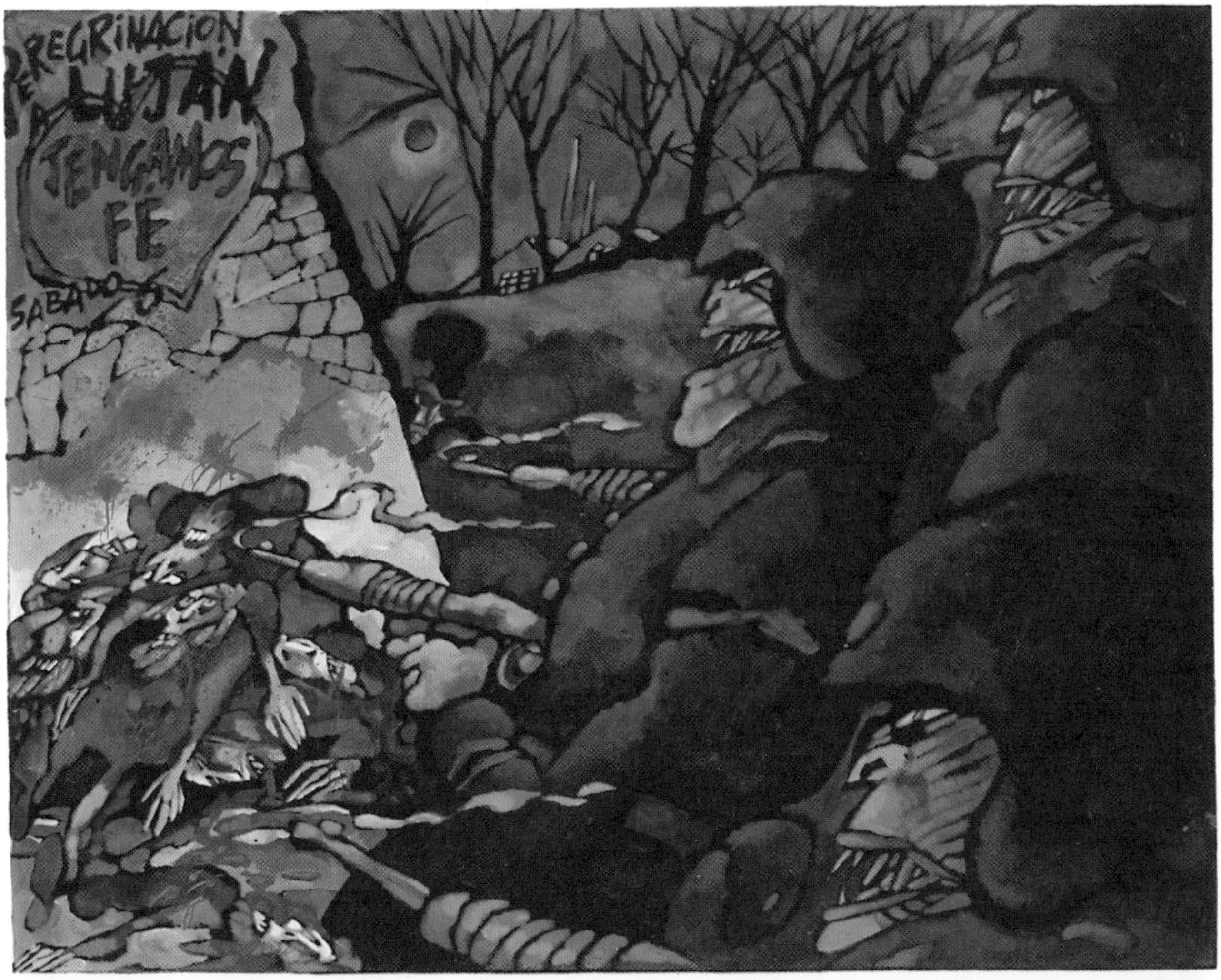
PEREGRINACION
A LUJAN
TENGAMOS
FE
SABADO 6

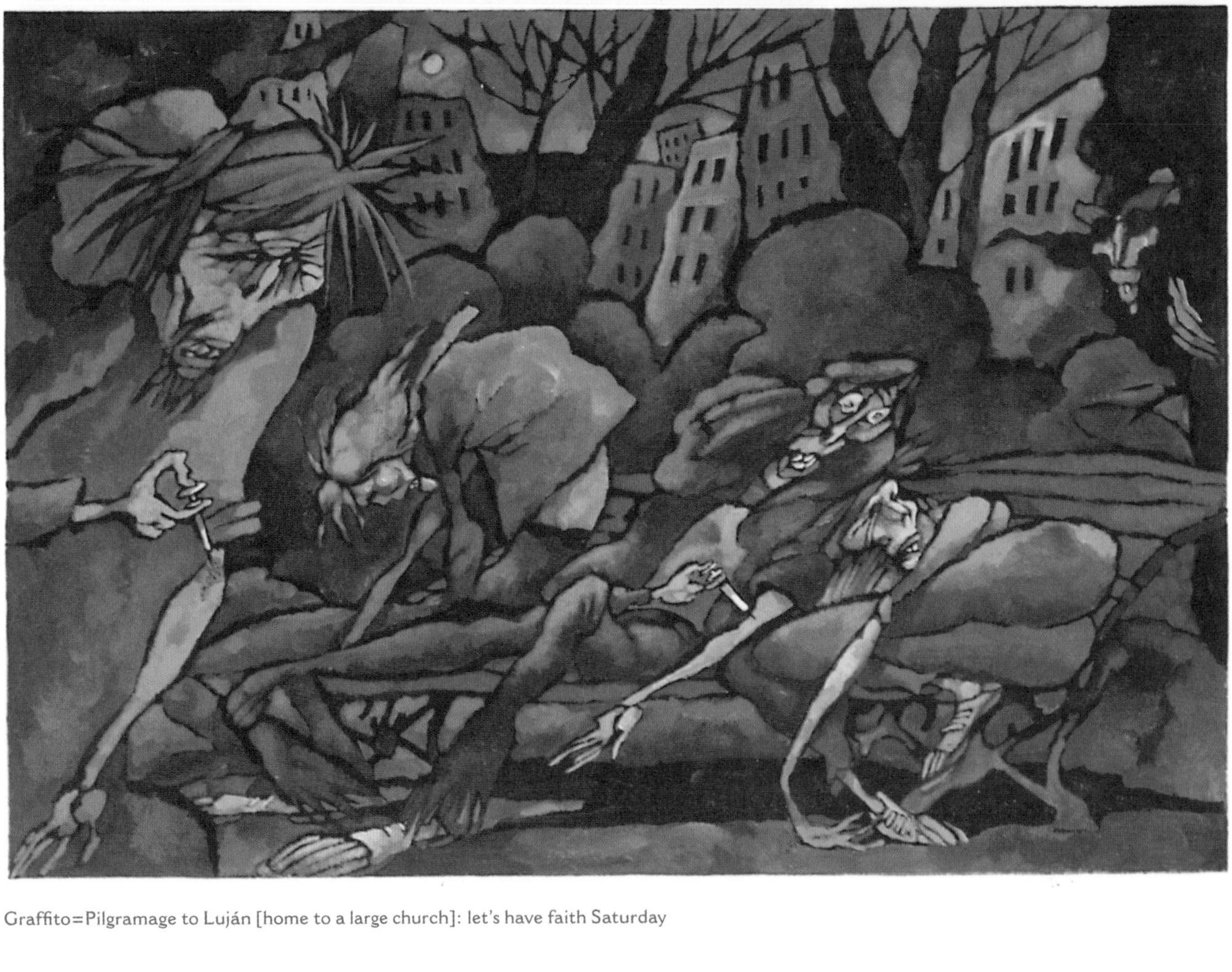

Graffito=Pilgramage to Luján [home to a large church]: let's have faith Saturday

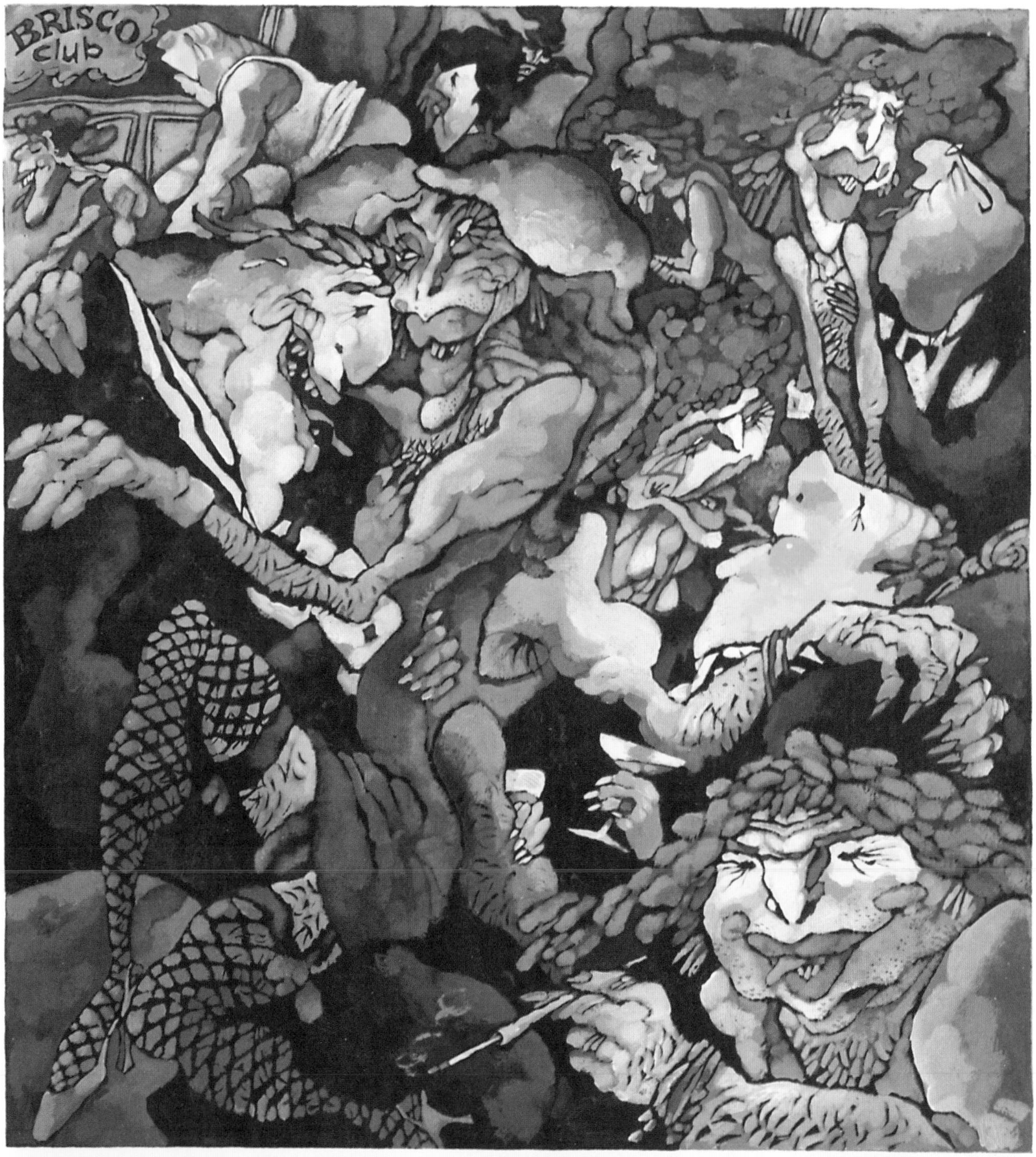
BRISCO
club

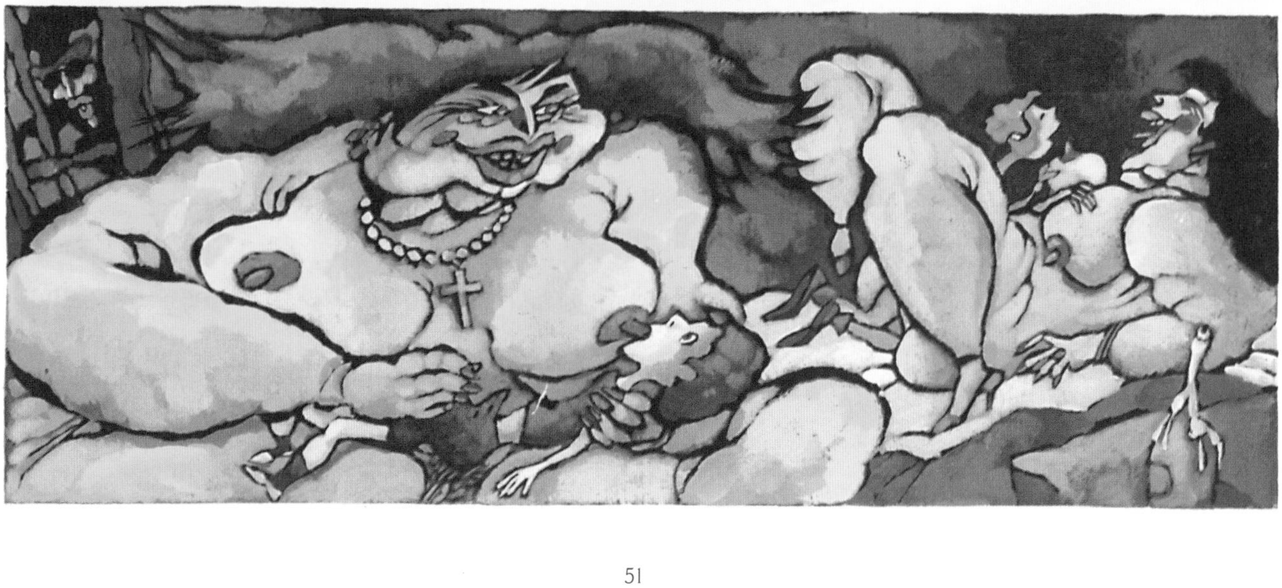

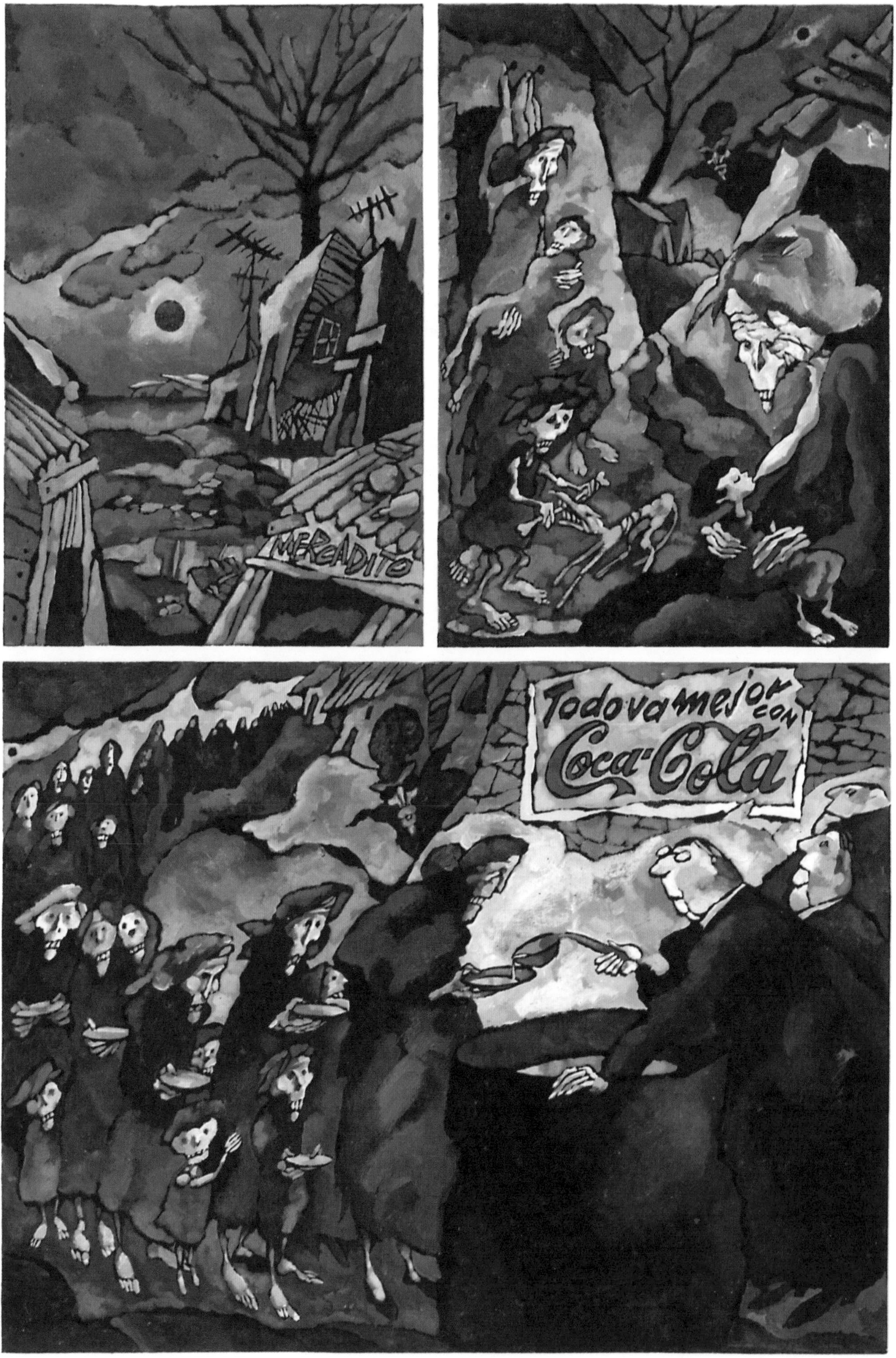
MERCADITO
Todo va mejor con
Coca-Cola

Mercadito: convenience store
todo va mejor con: Things go Better with Coca Cola

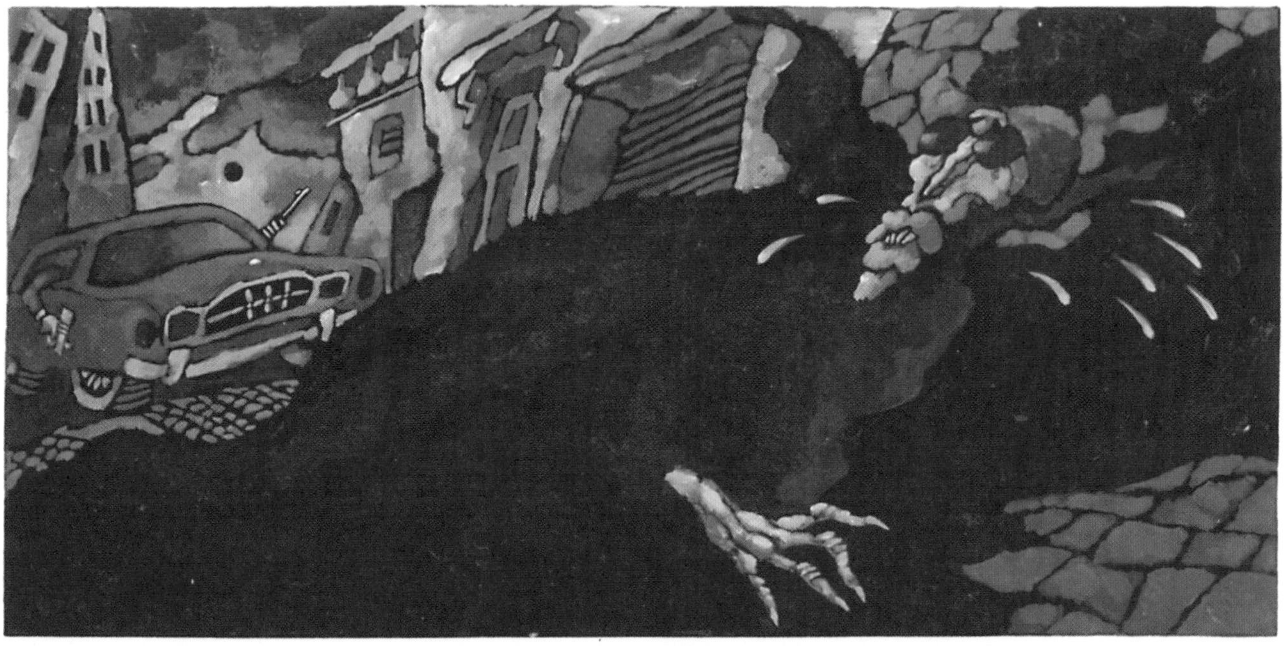

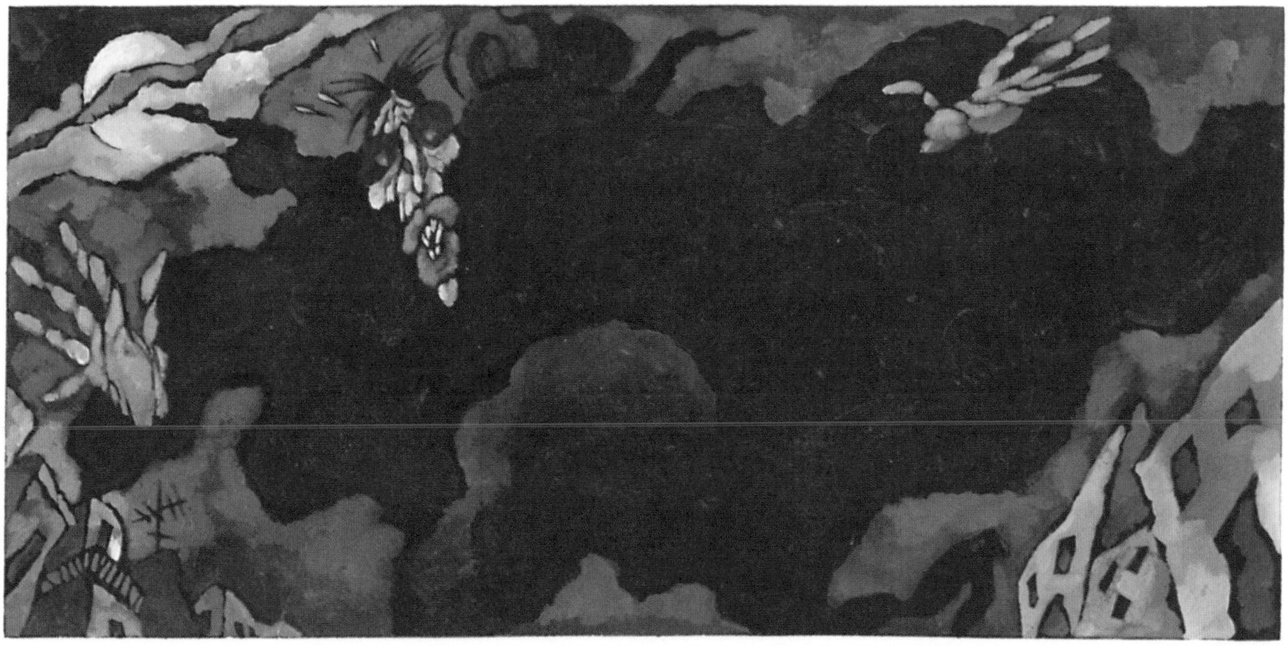

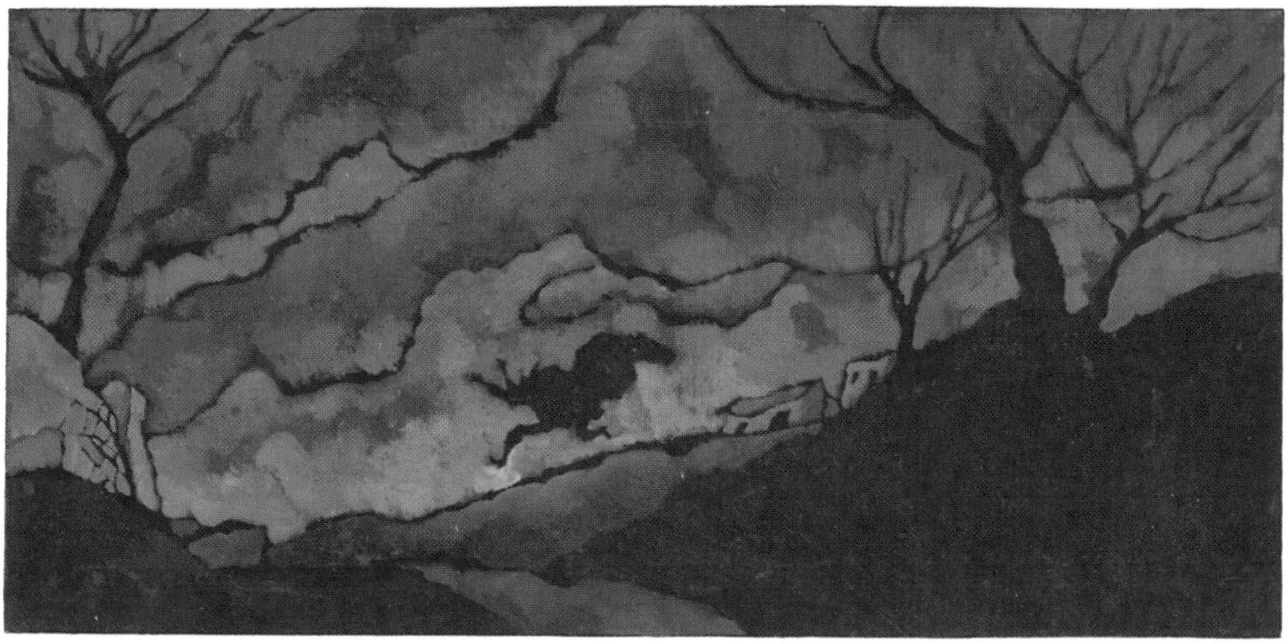

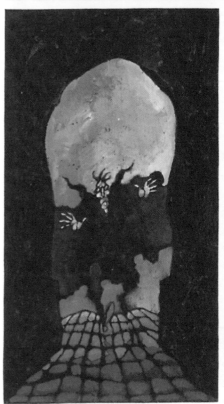

FIVE

Poe? Yuck!

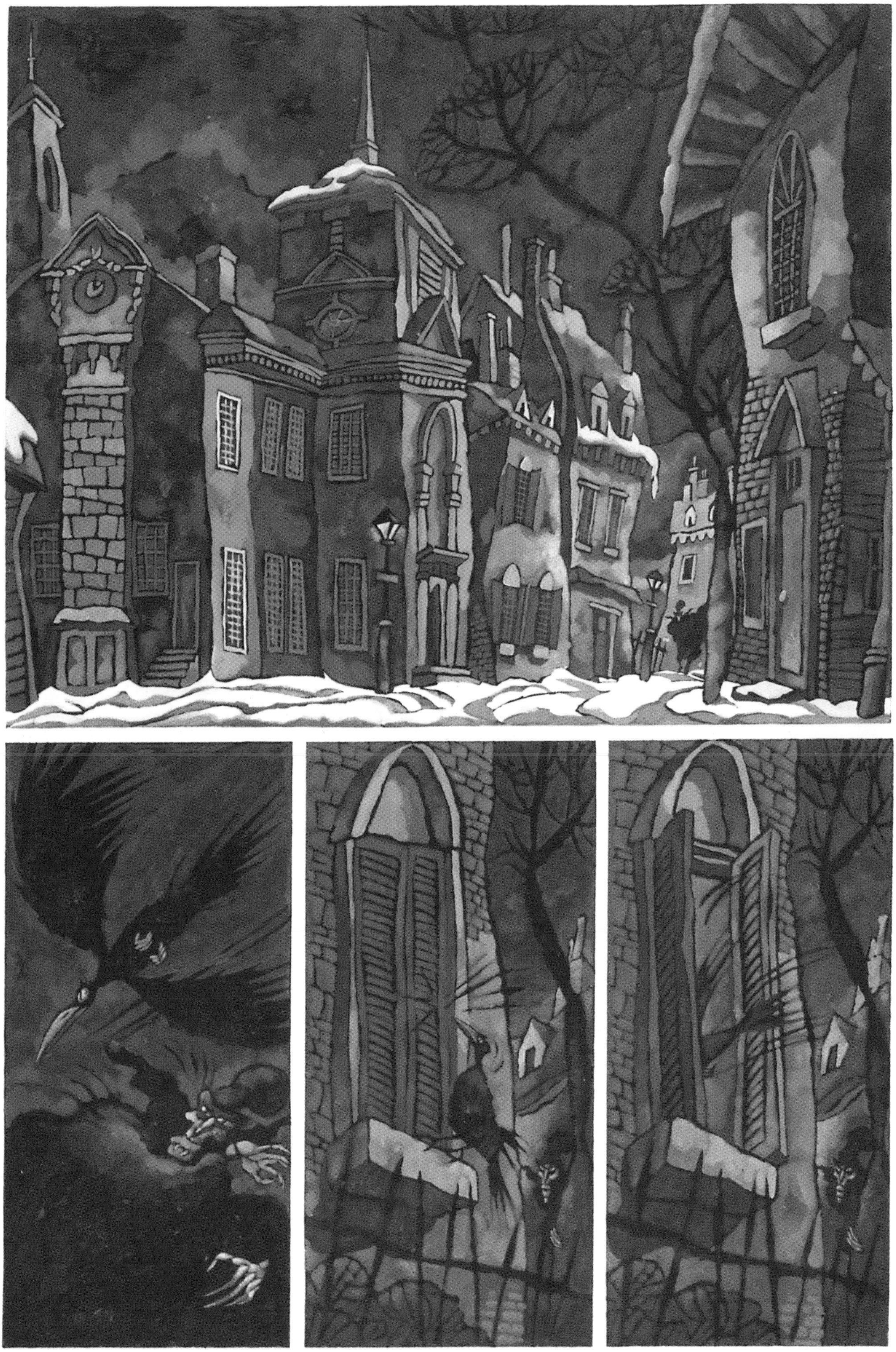

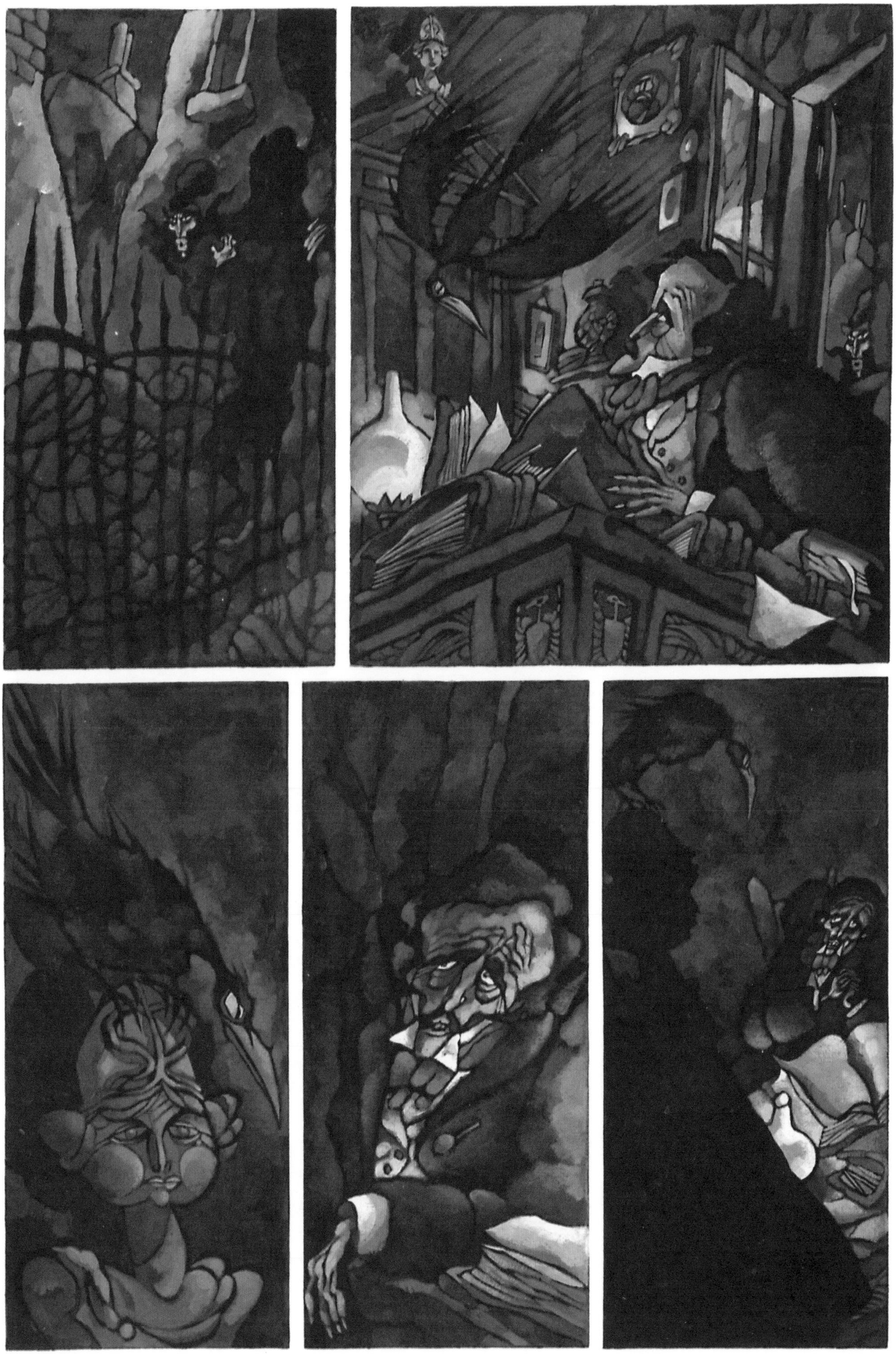

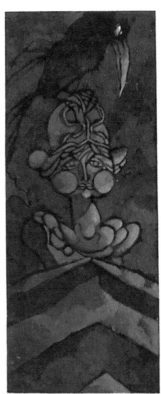

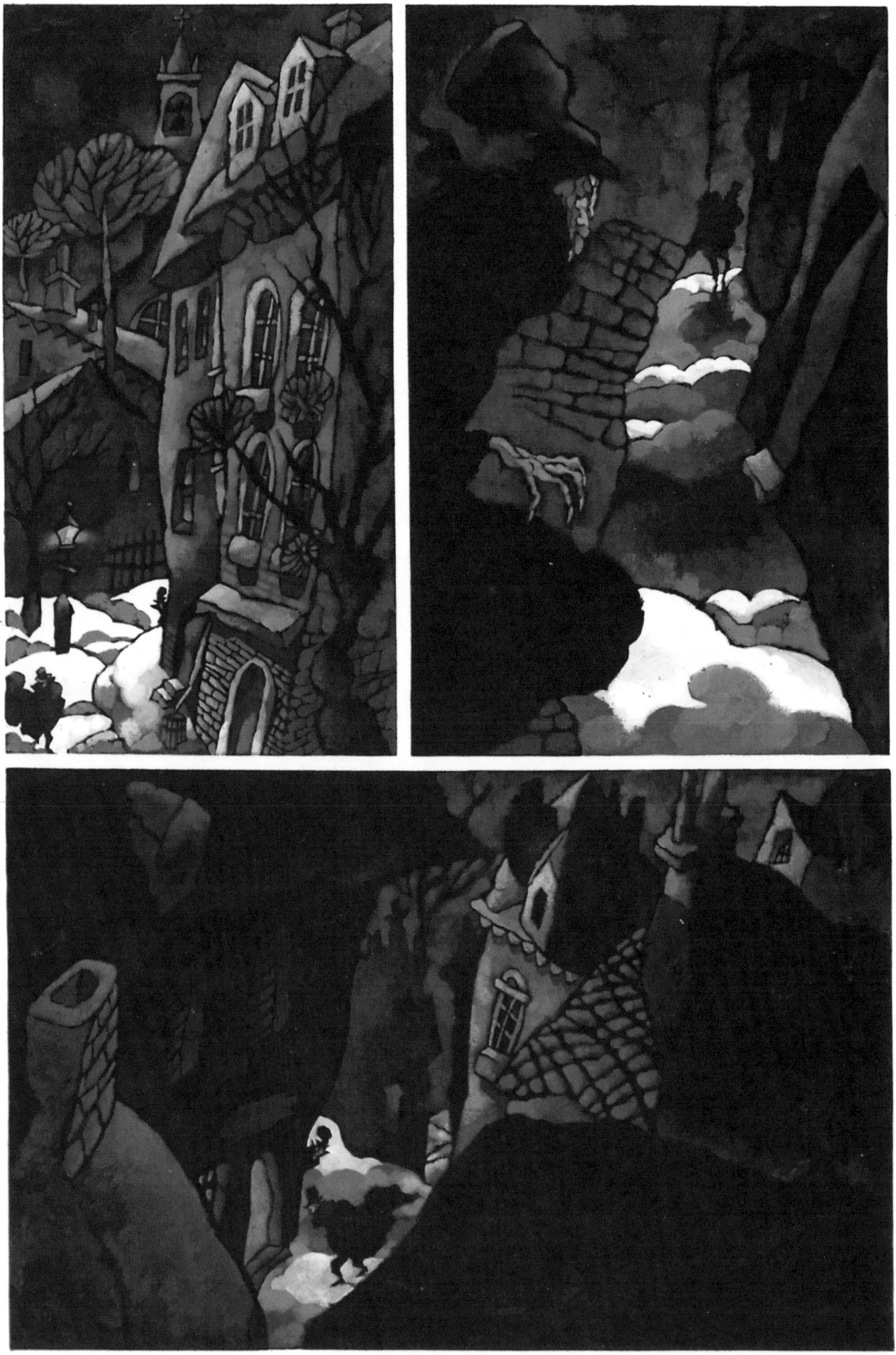

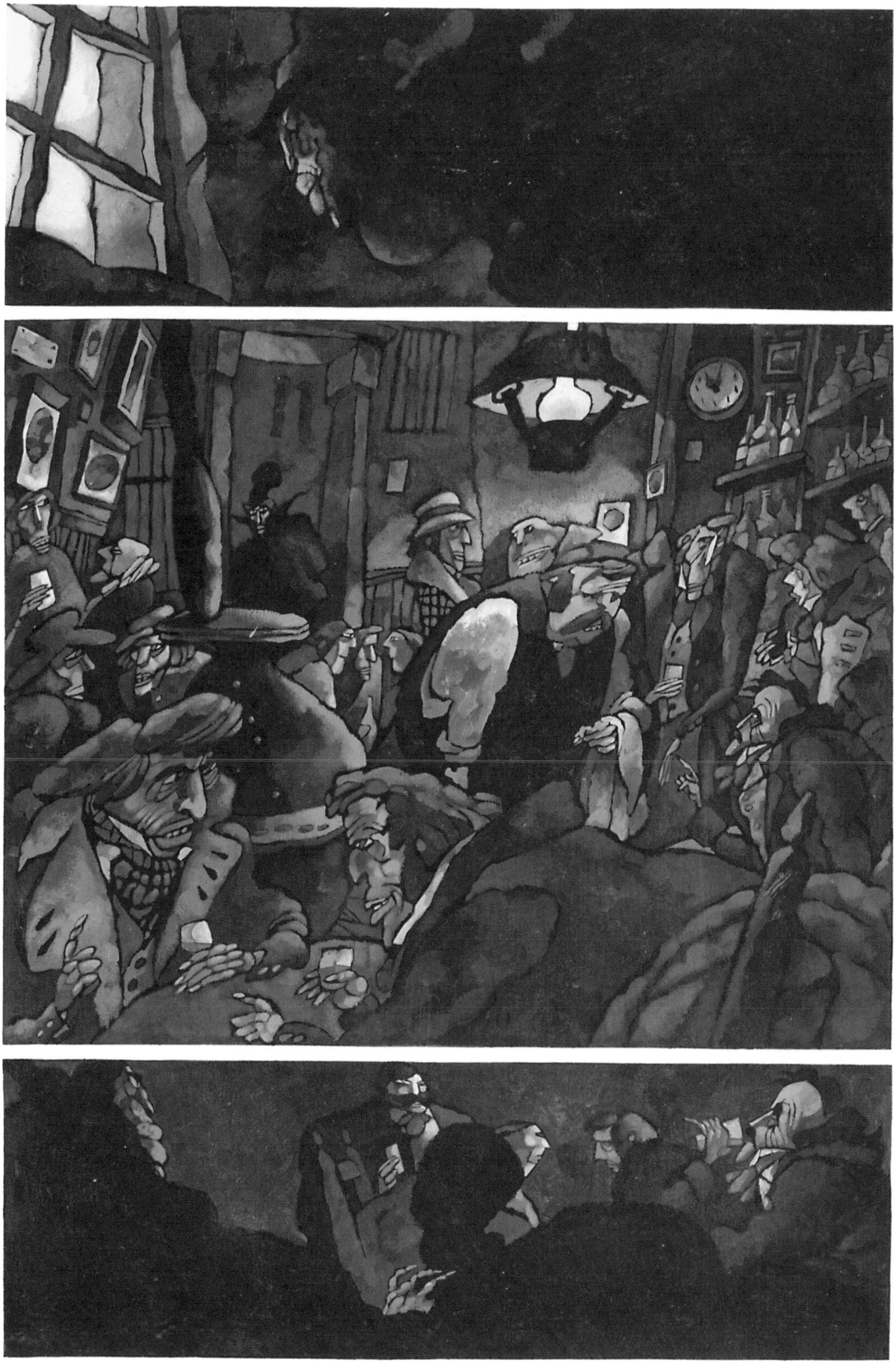

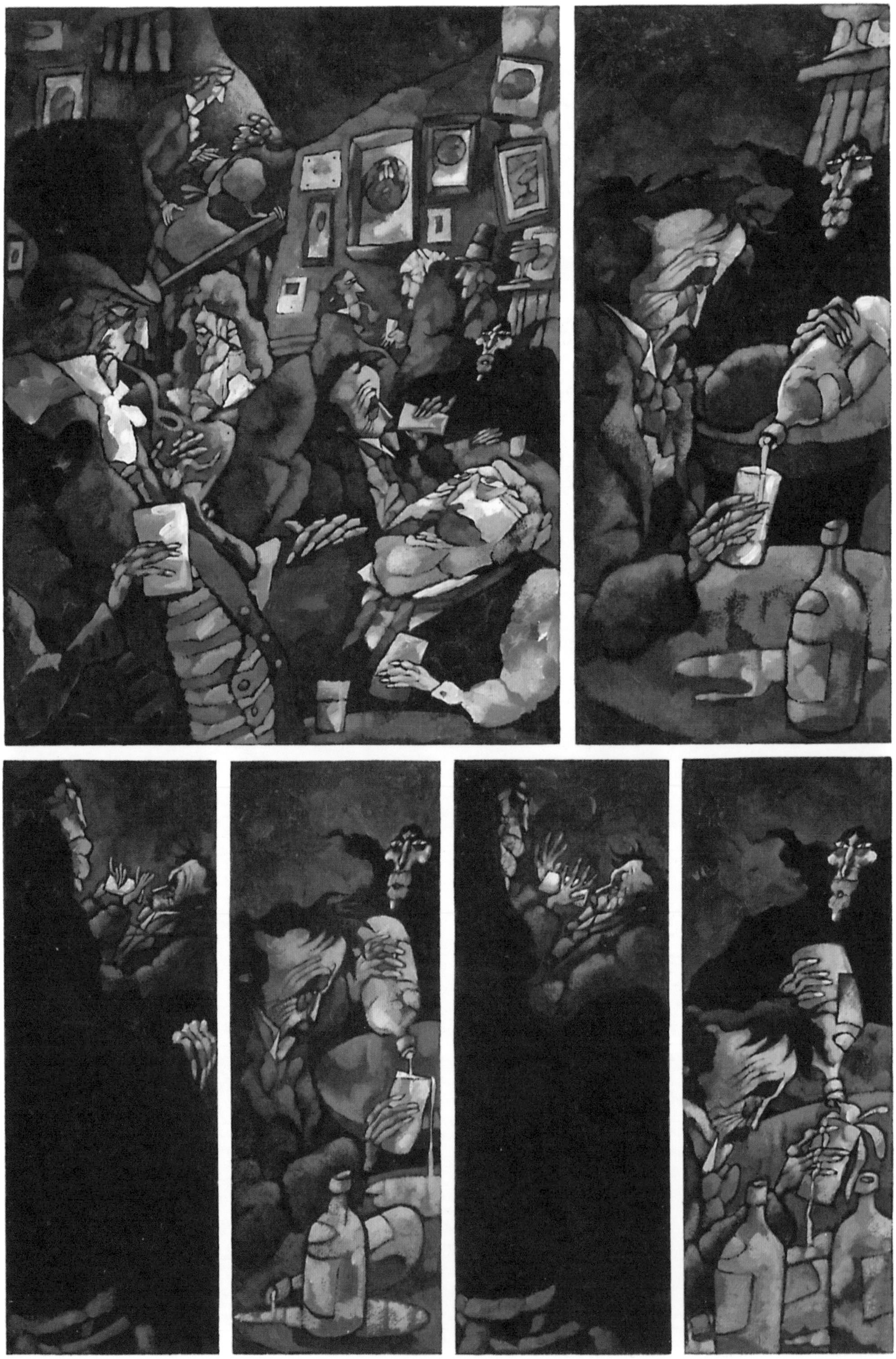

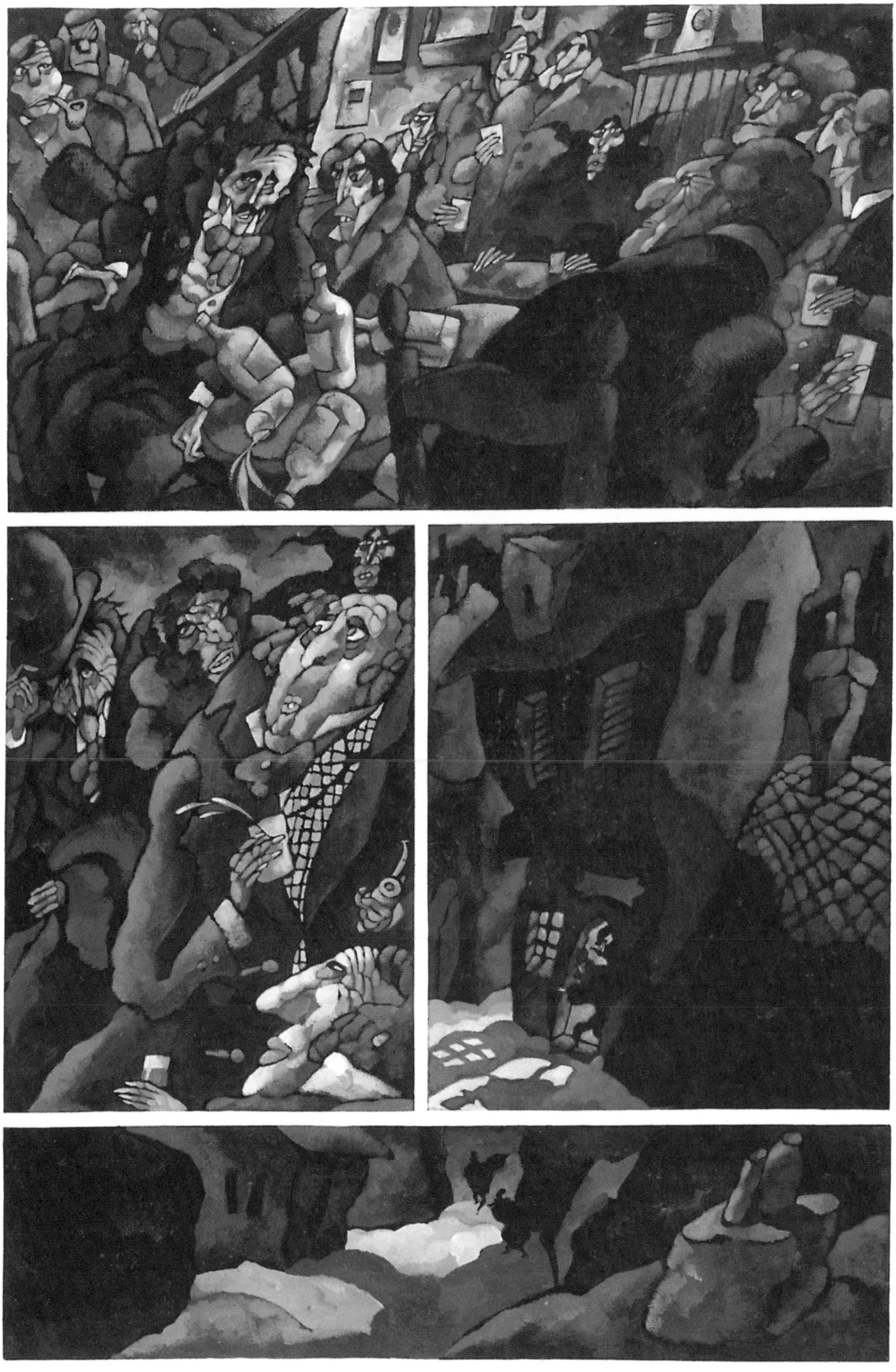

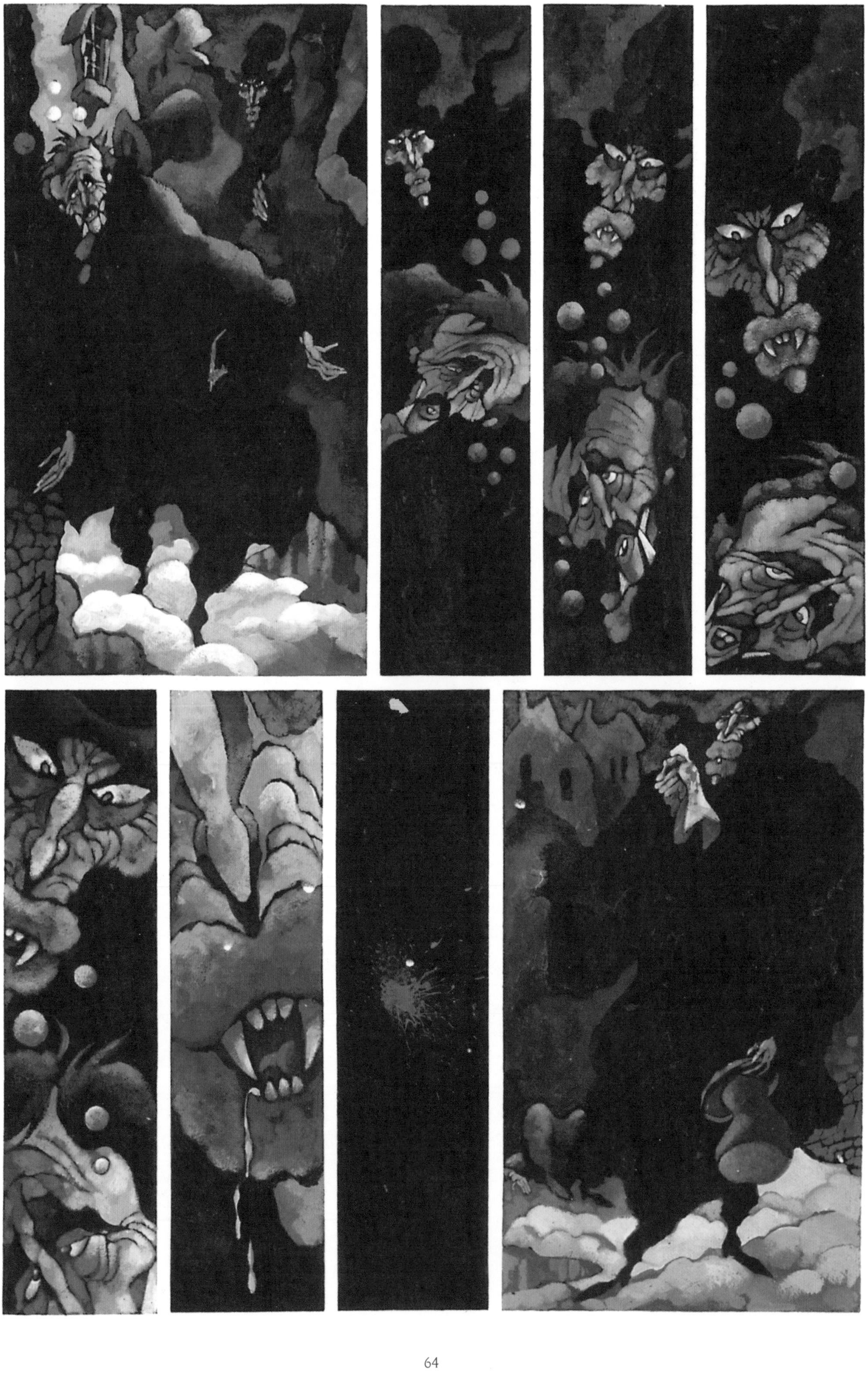

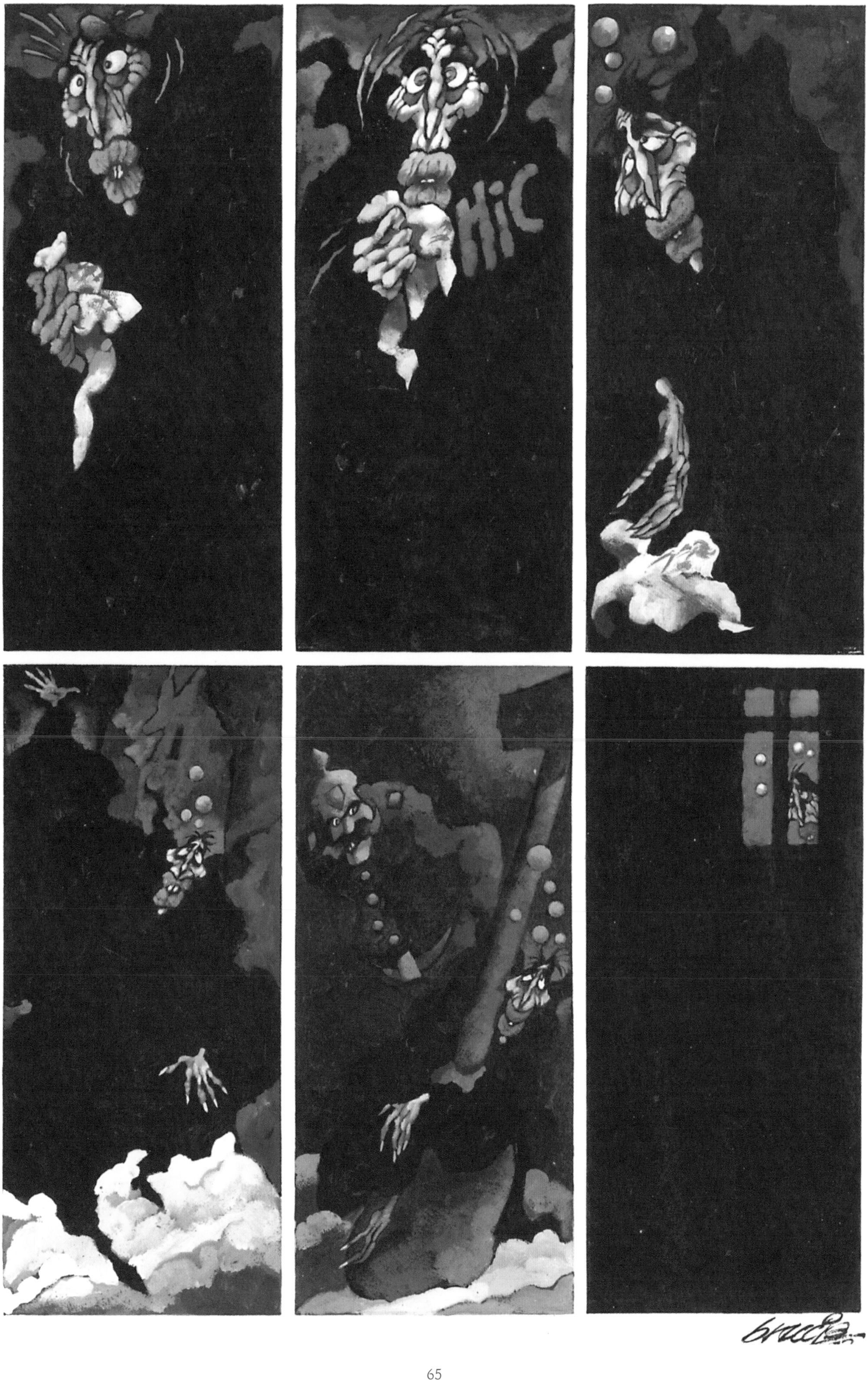
HIC

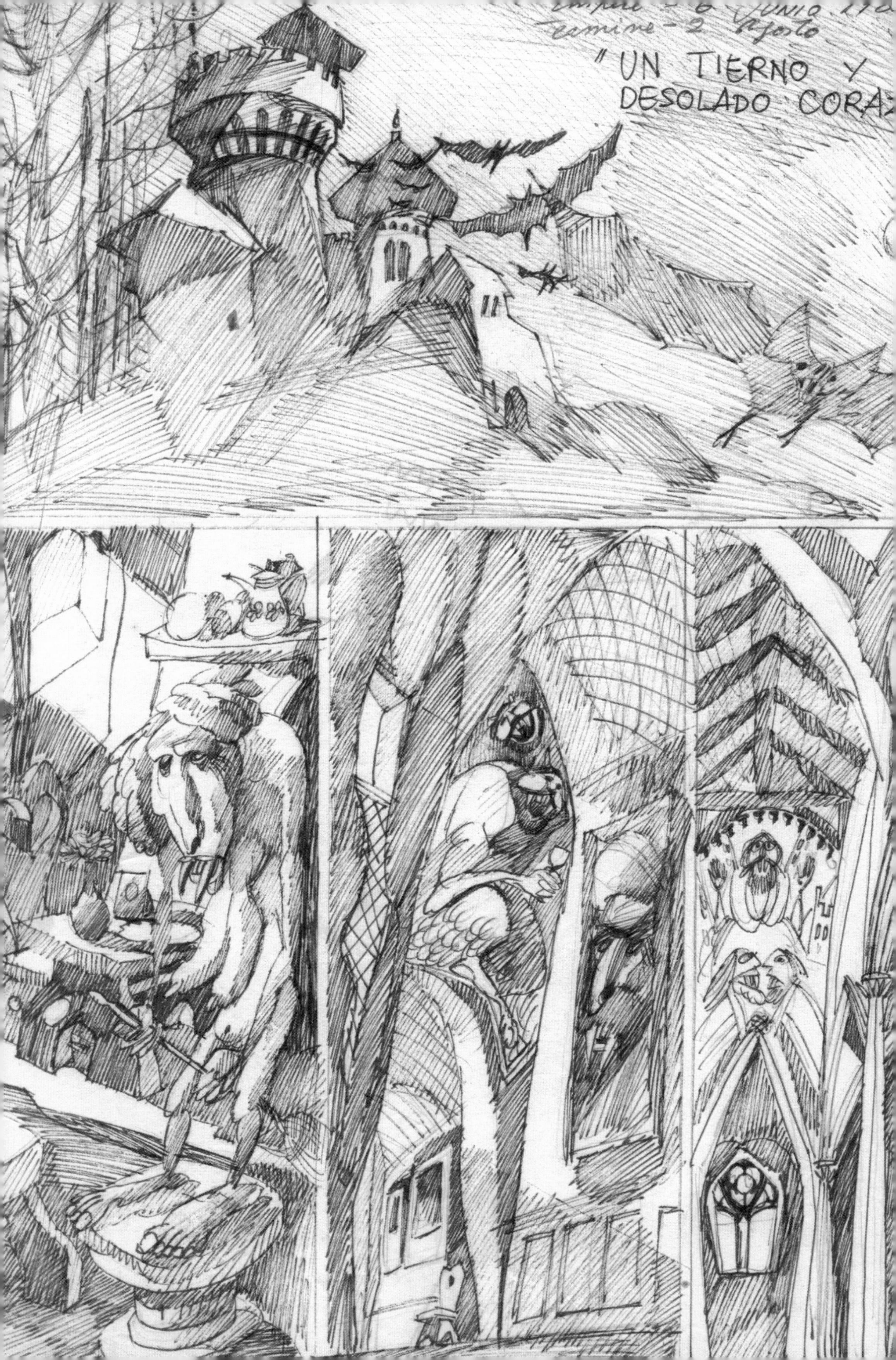
"UN TIERNO Y DESOLADO CORAZ

SKETCHBOOK

La ultima noche de Carnaval
Venecia
Boceto original año 1981

Empezé el martes 23 febrero 1983
Termini Lunes 21 mayo 1983
La ultima noche de Carnaval
PAG. 1

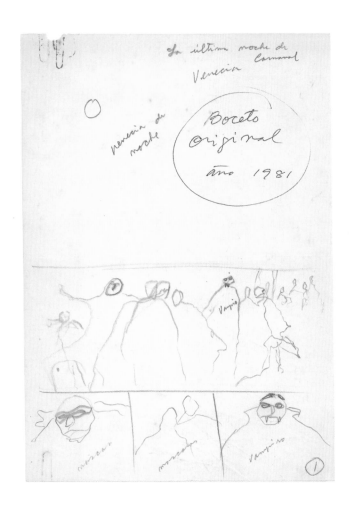

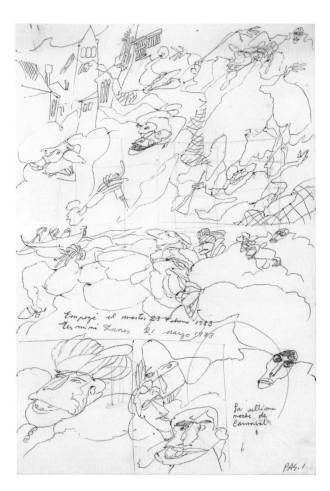

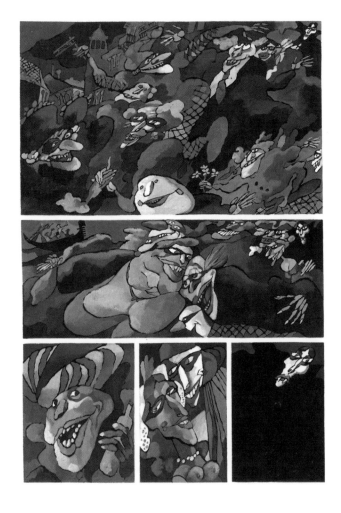

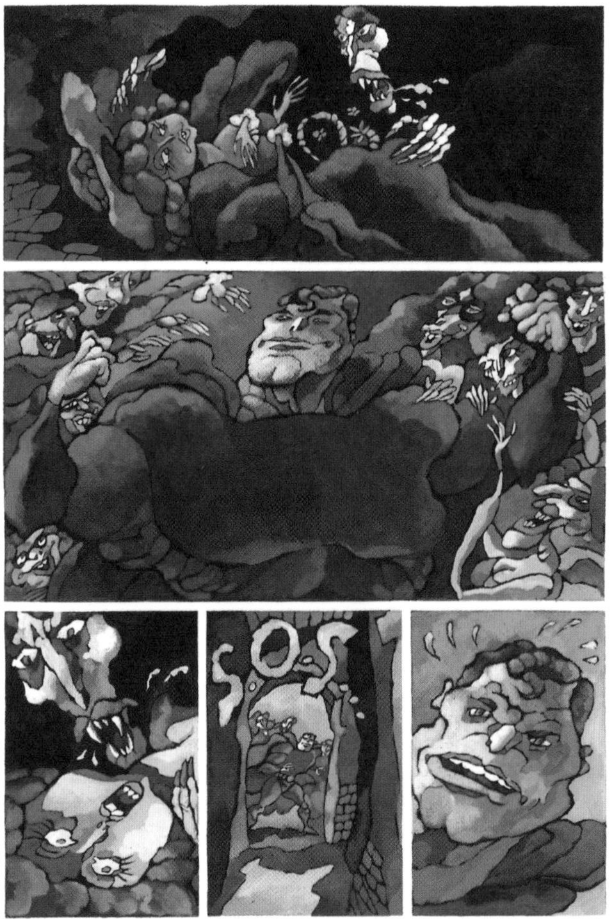
S.O.S

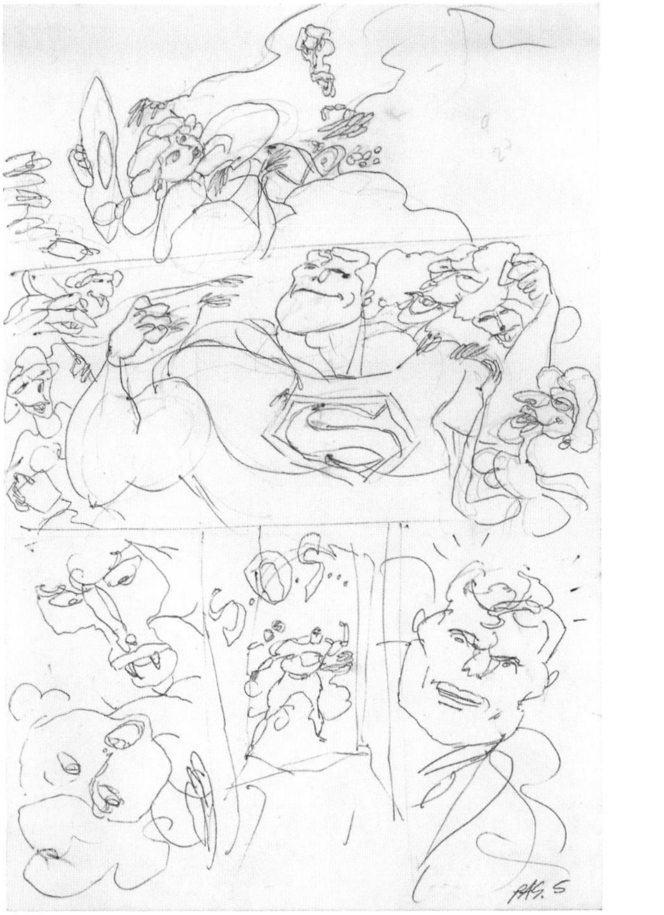
S.O.S...

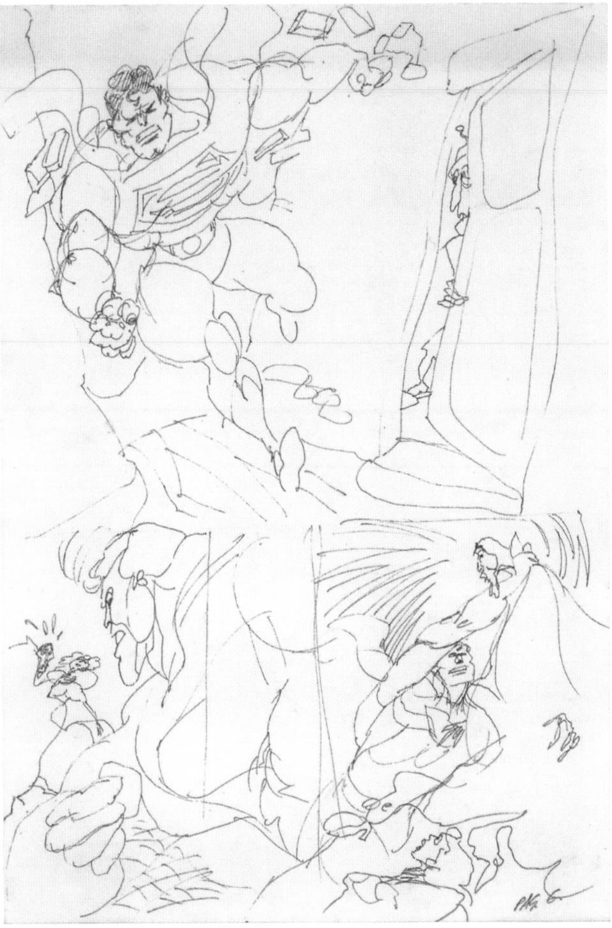

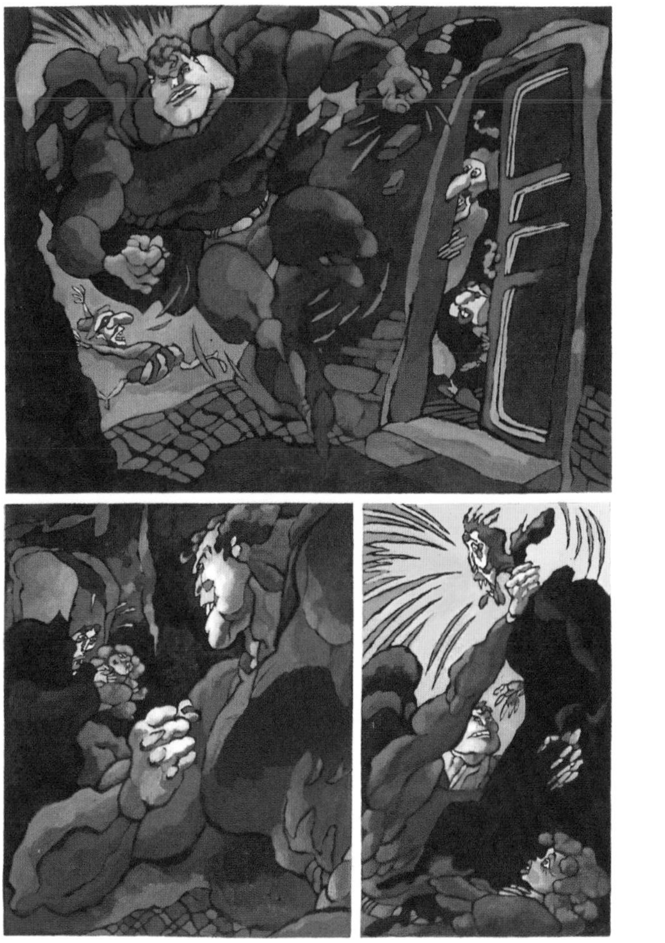

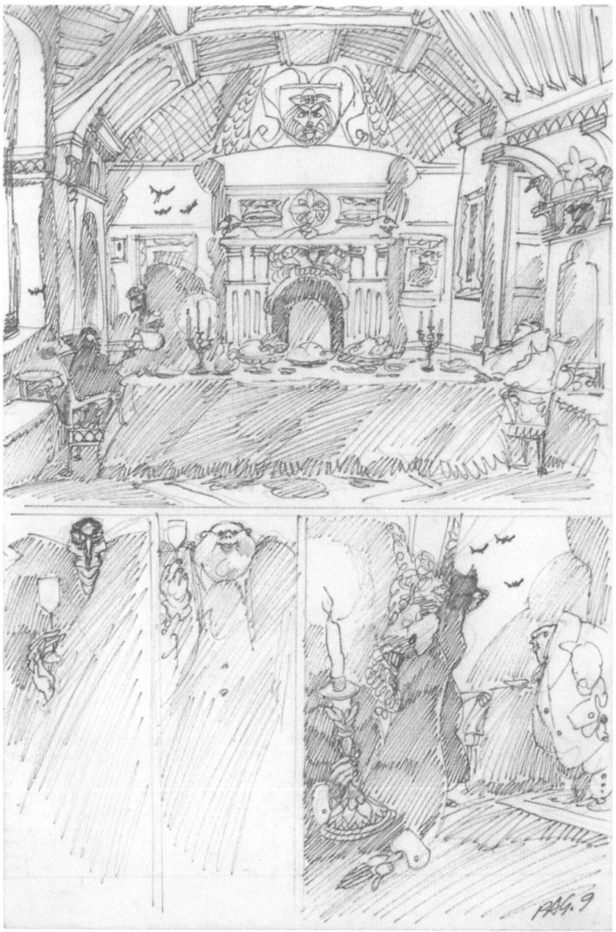
PAG. 9

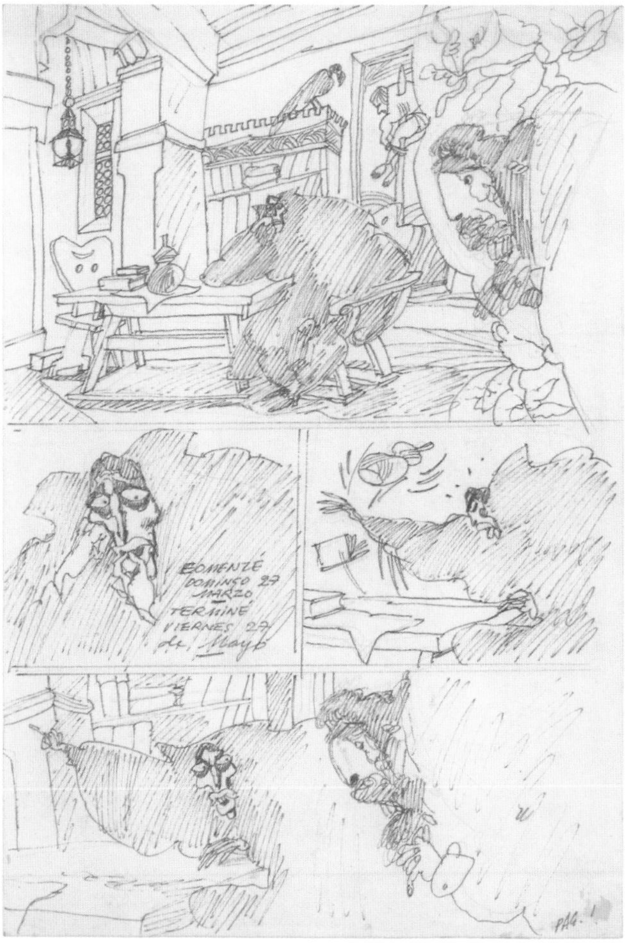
COMENZÉ
DOMINGO 27
MARZO
TERMINÉ
VIERNES 27
de Mayo
PAG. 1

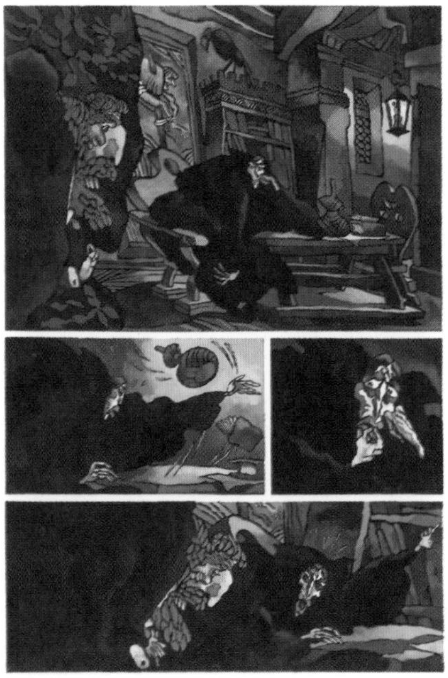

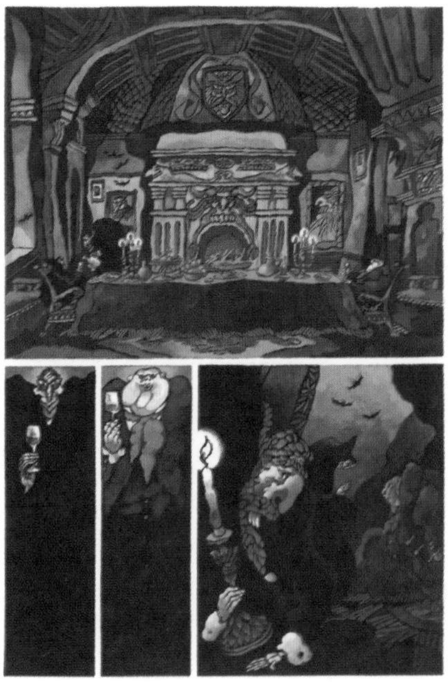

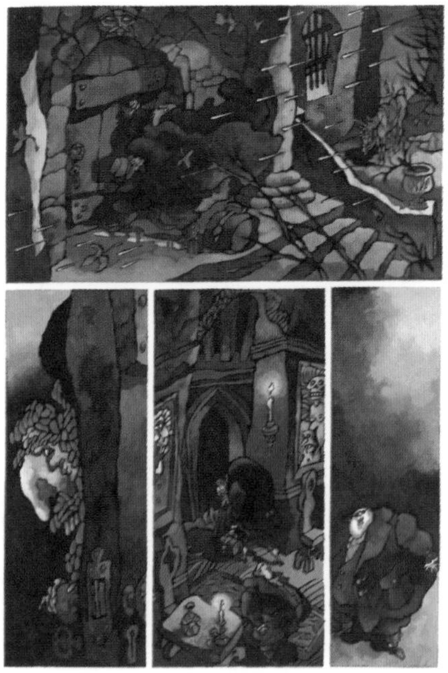

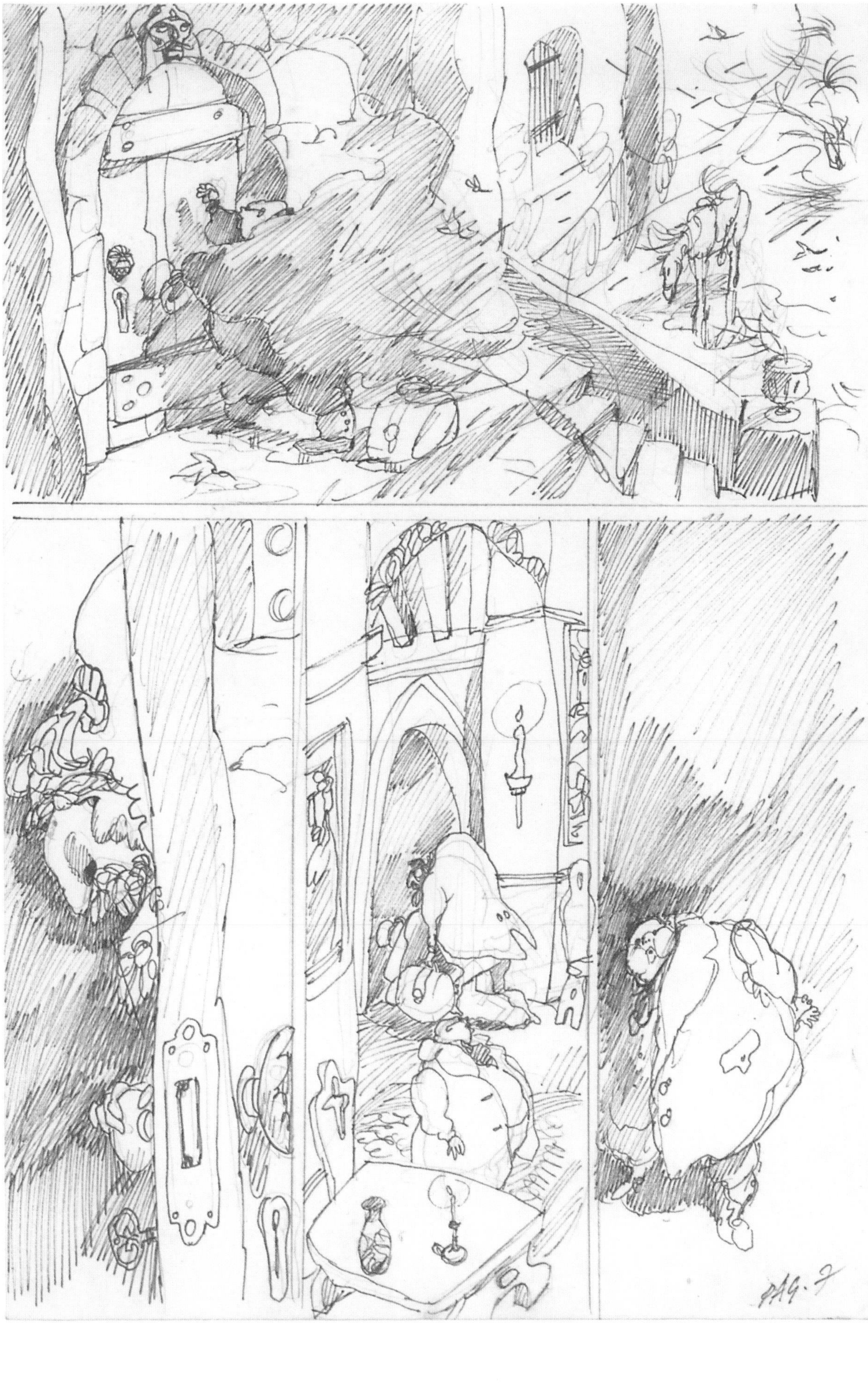
PAG. 9

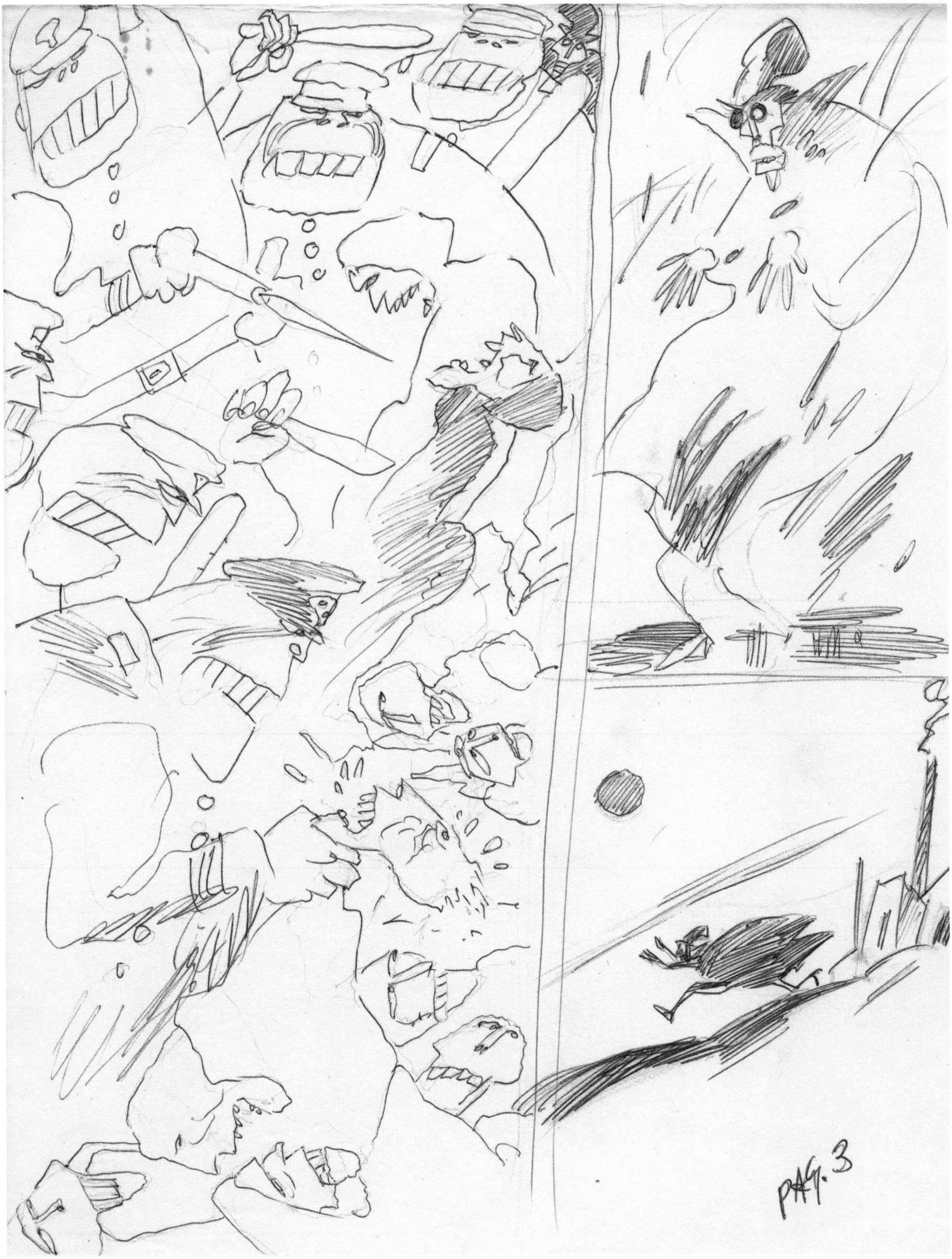
PAG. 3

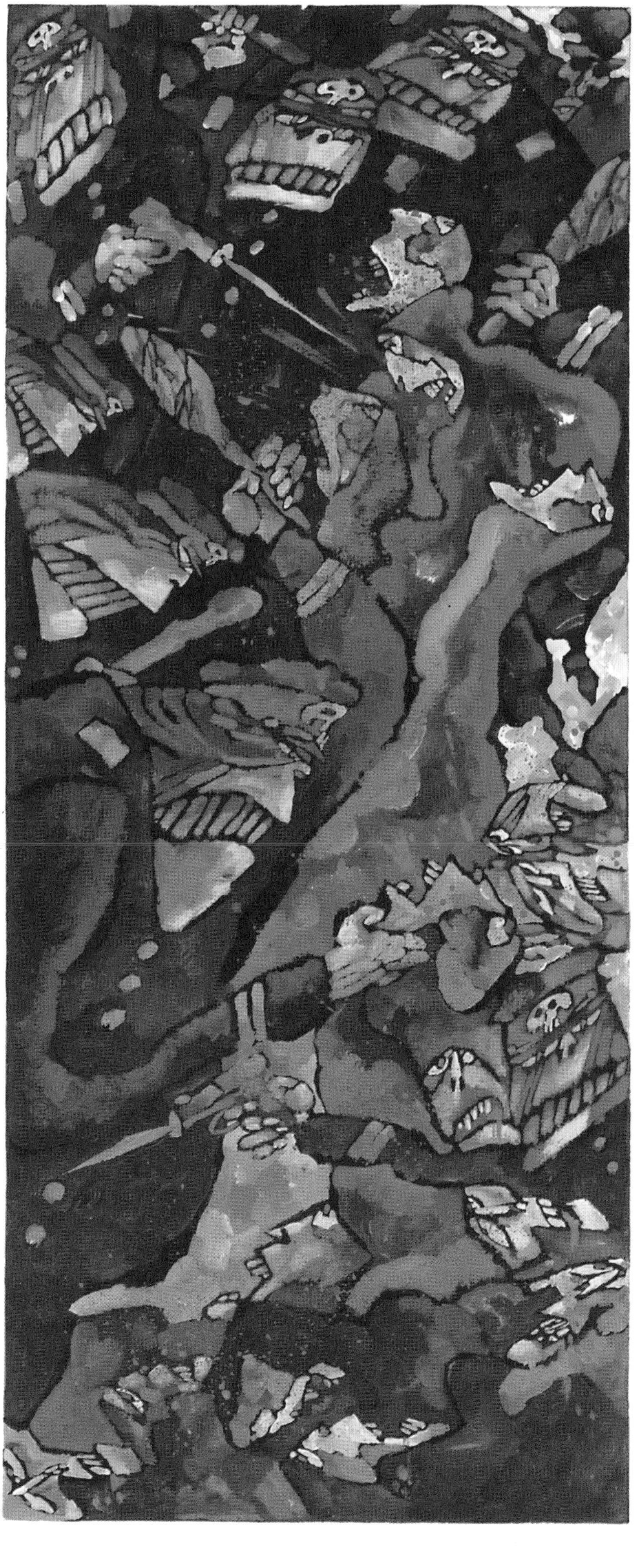
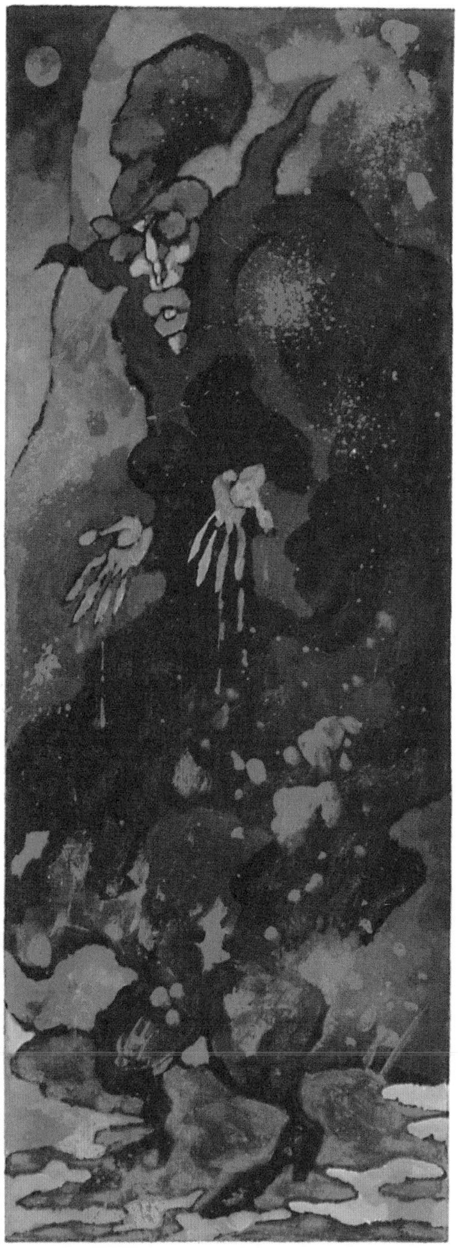
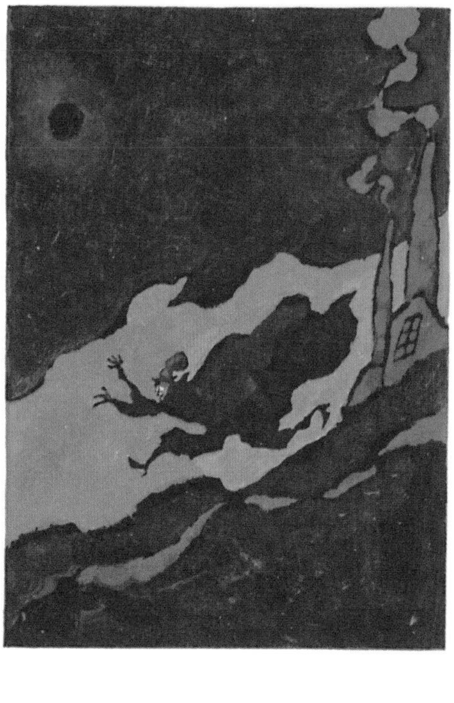

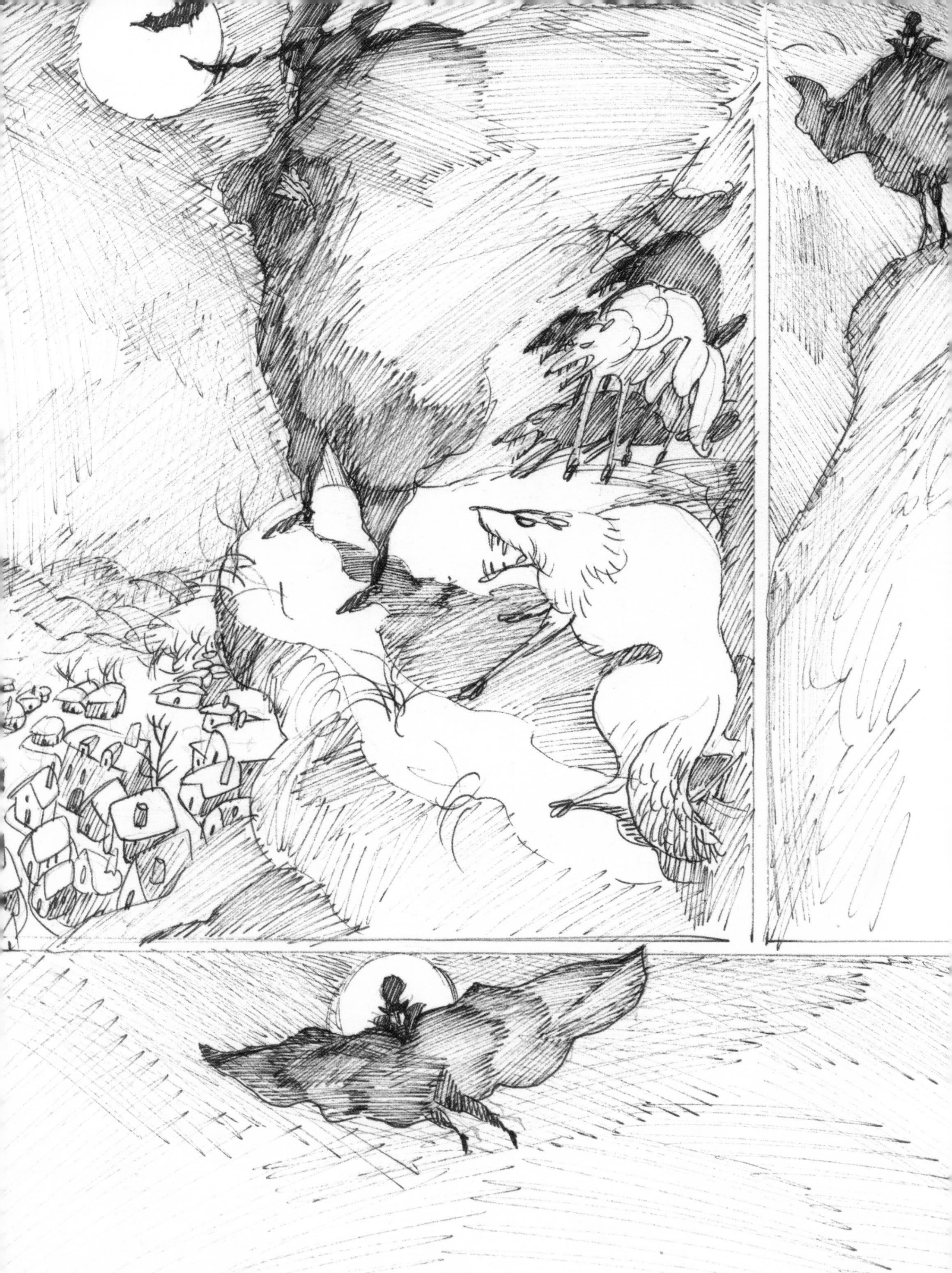

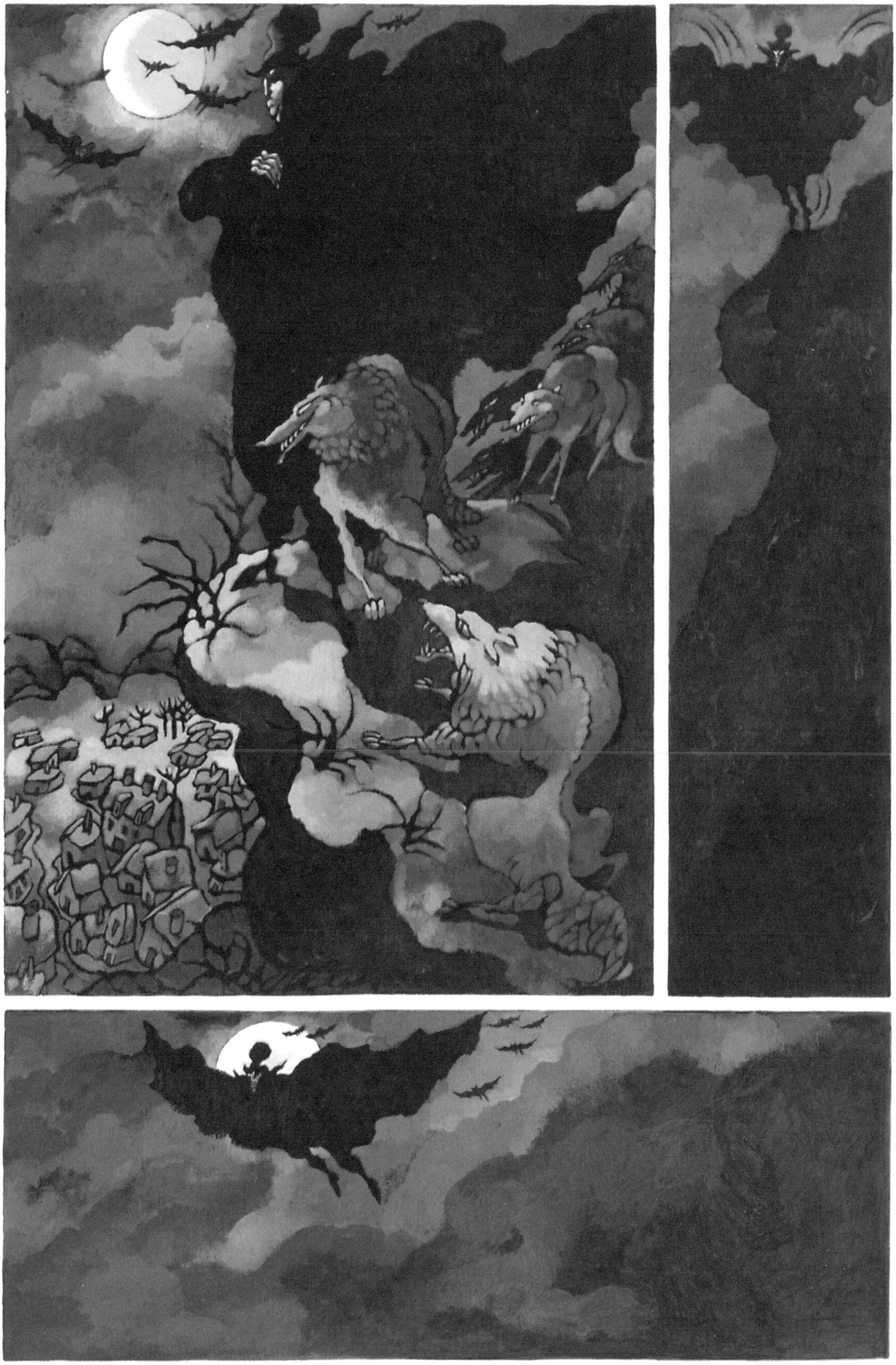

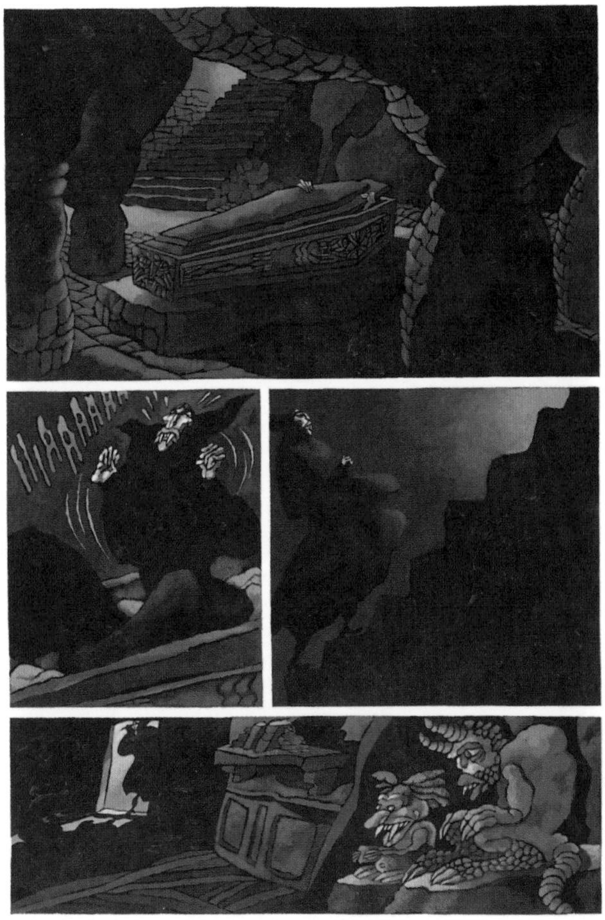

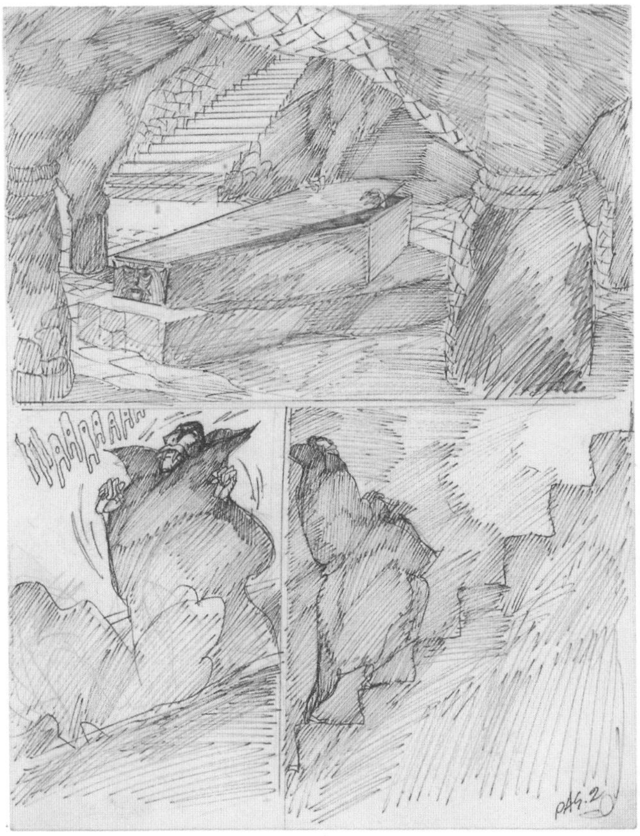
PAG.2

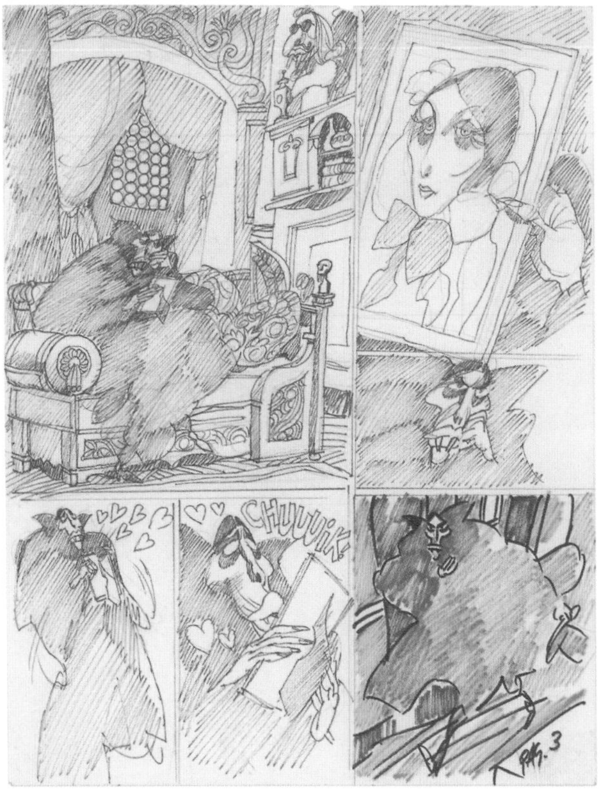
CHUUUIK!
PAG.3

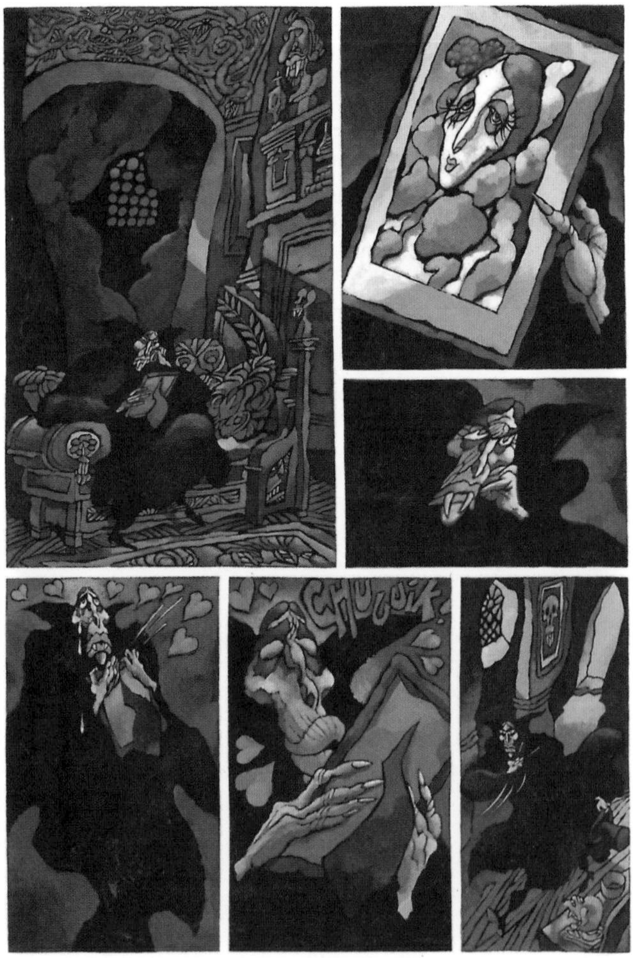

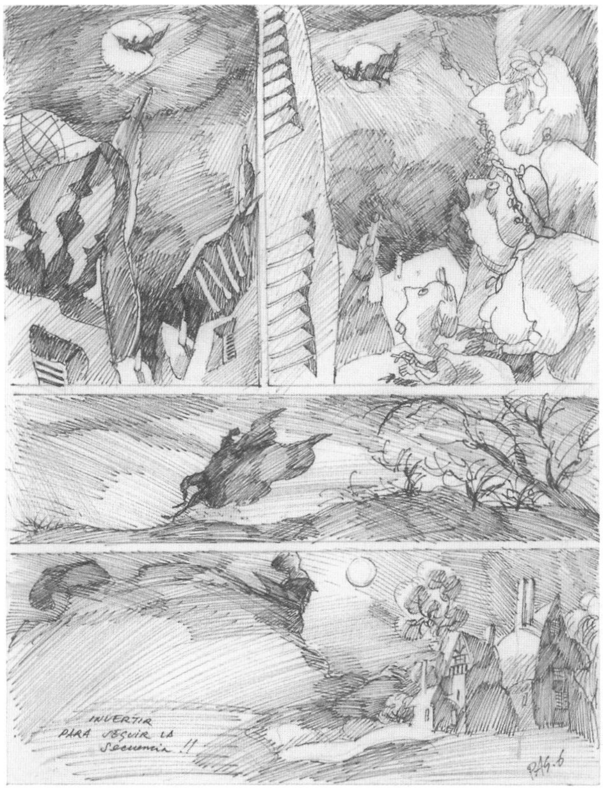
INVERTIR
PARA SEGUIR LA
Secuencia !!

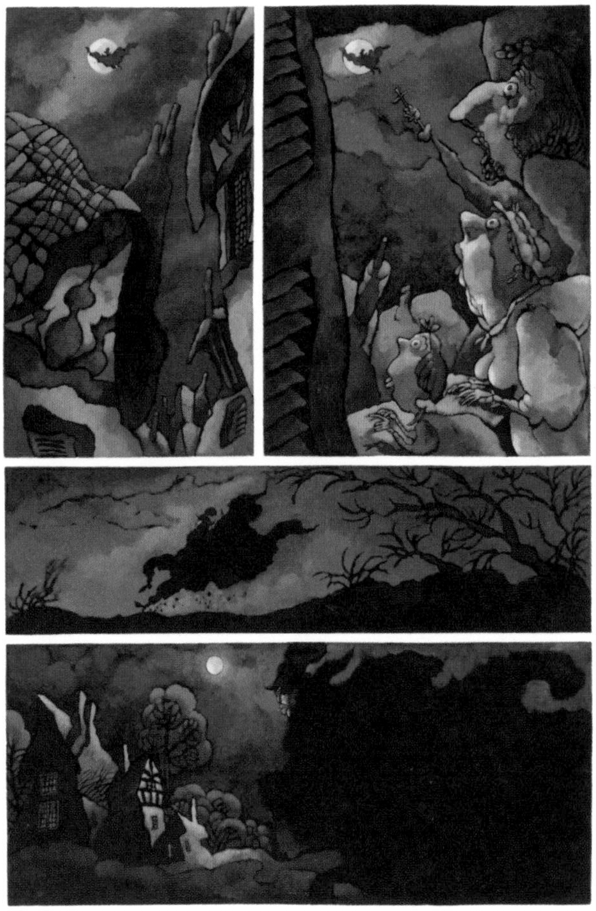

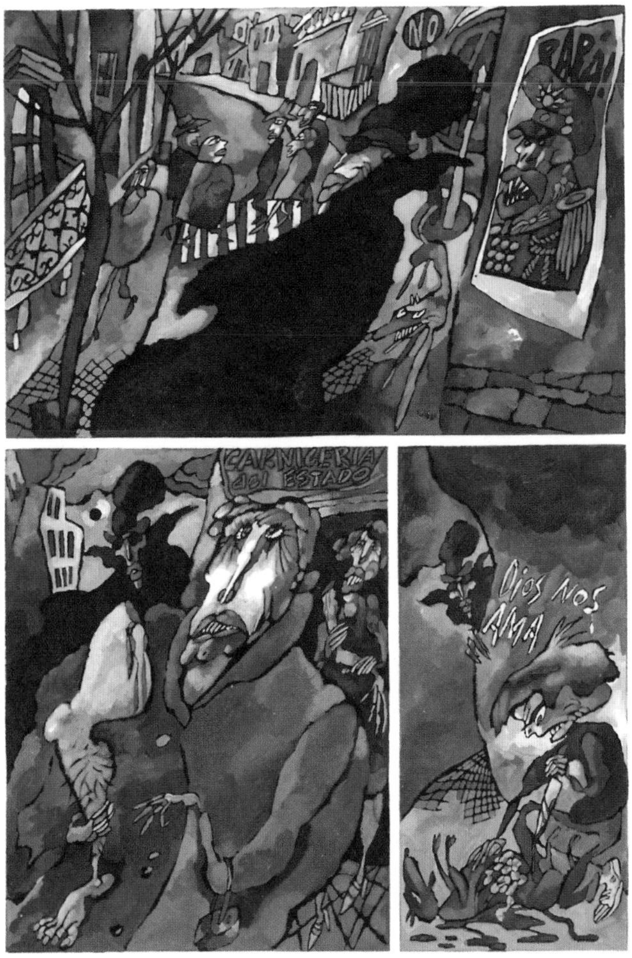
NO
CARNICERIA del ESTADO
DIOS NOS AMA

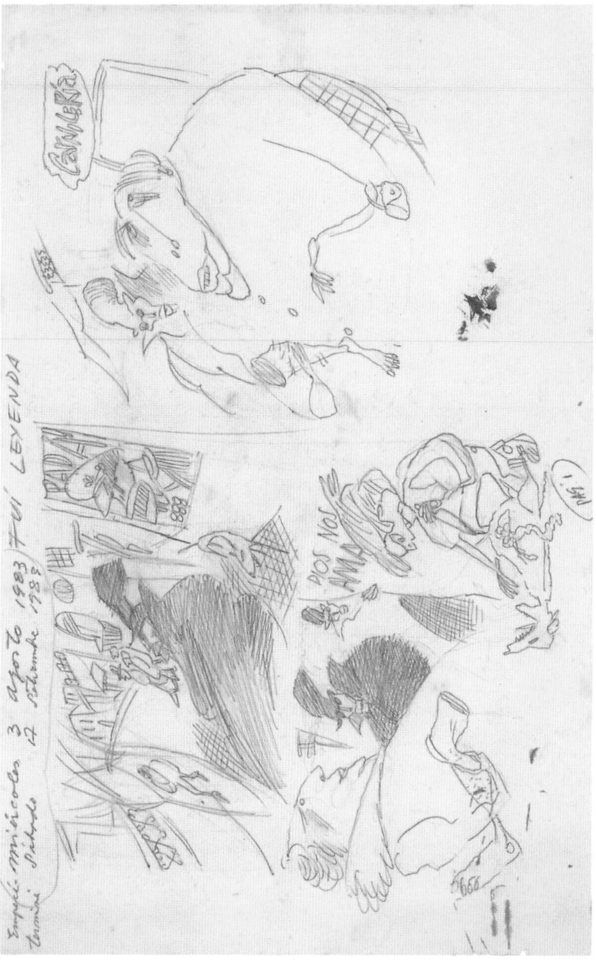
FUI LEYENDA
DIOS NOS AMA

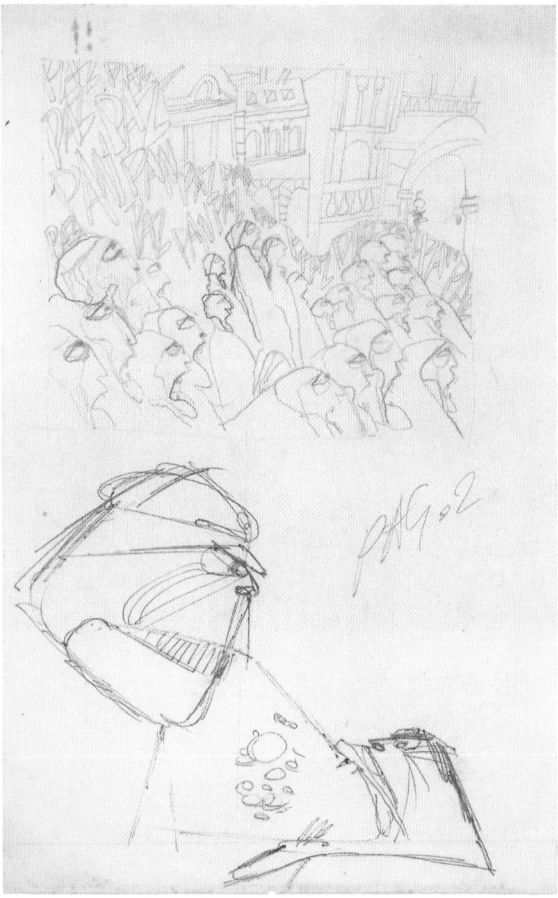
PAG. 2

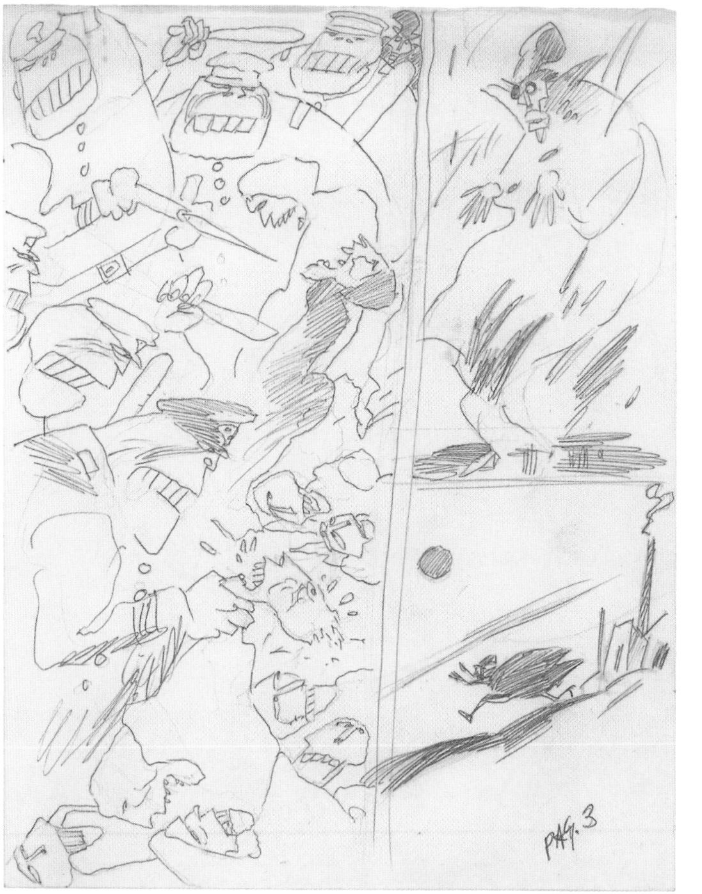
PAG. 3

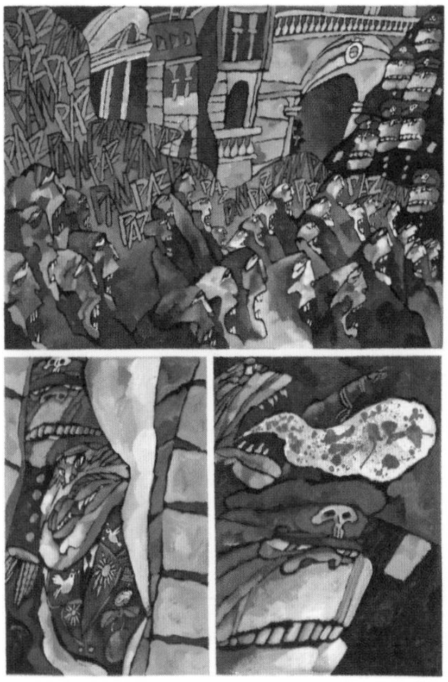

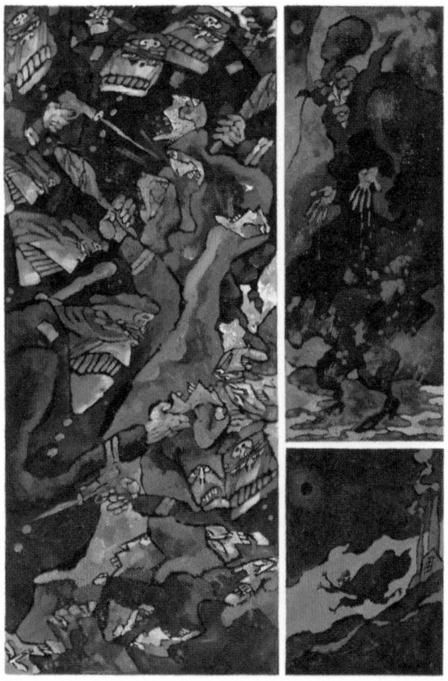

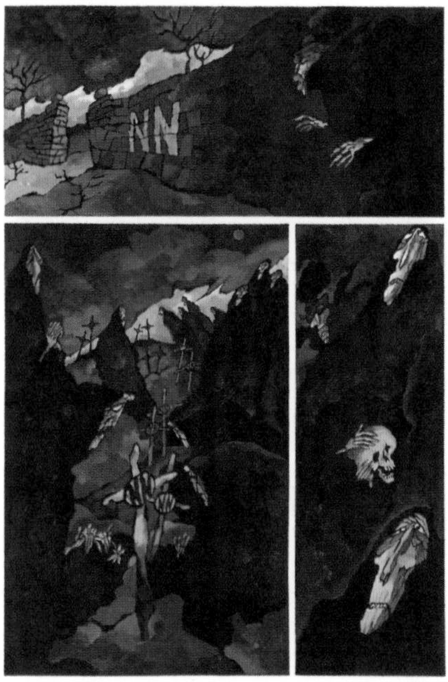
NN

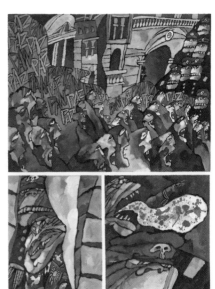

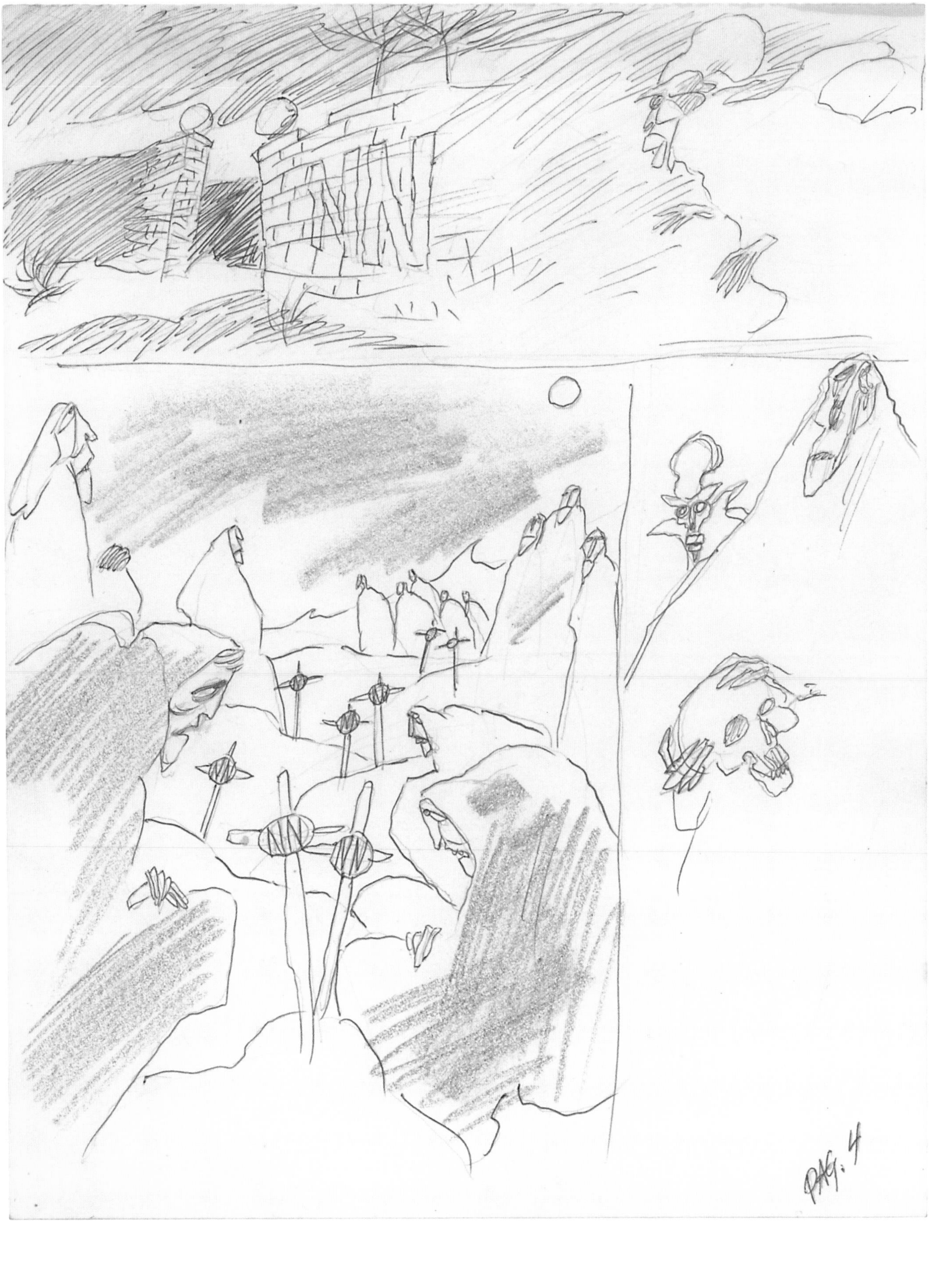
PAG. 4

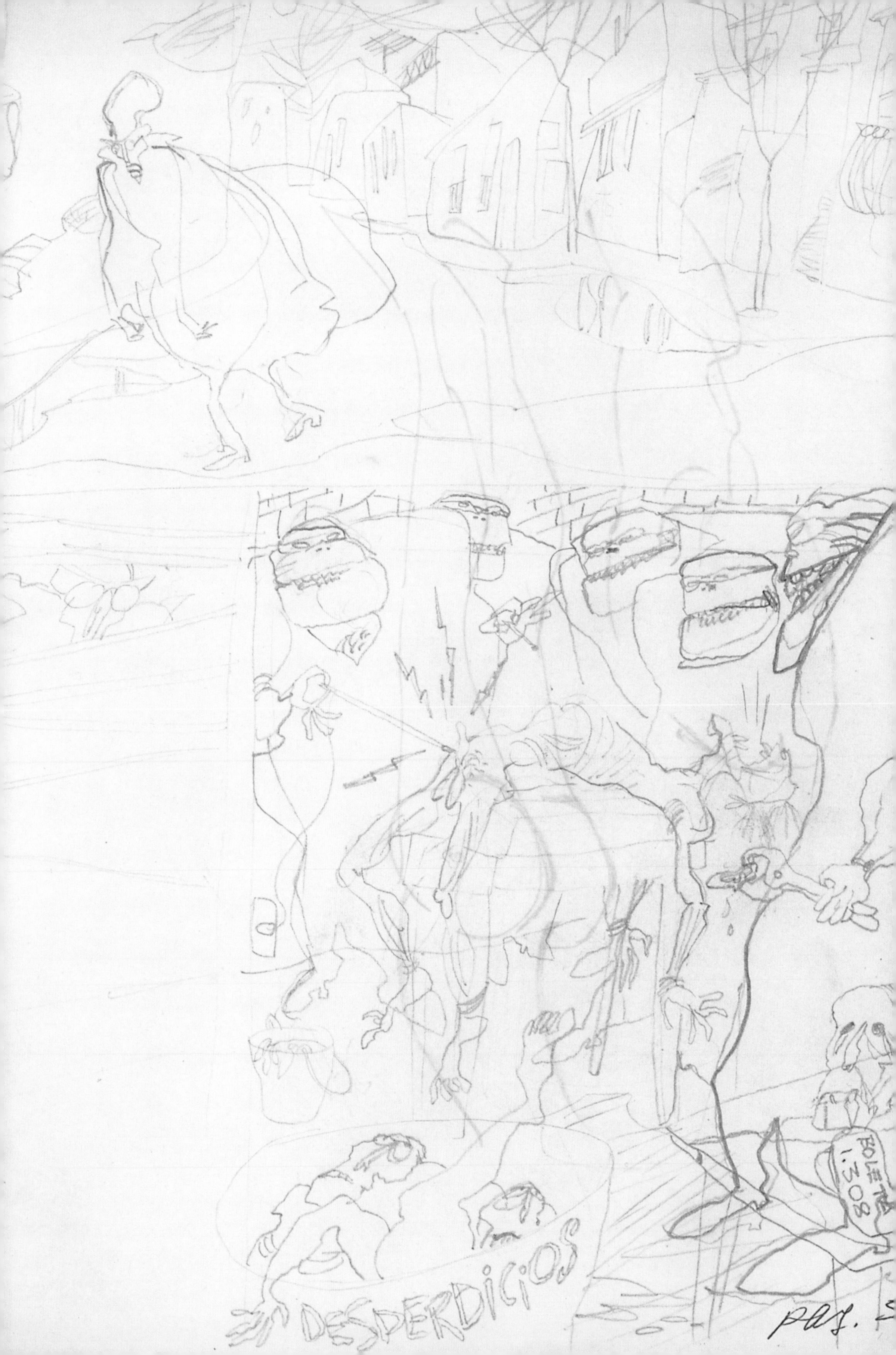
DESPERDICIOS
1.308

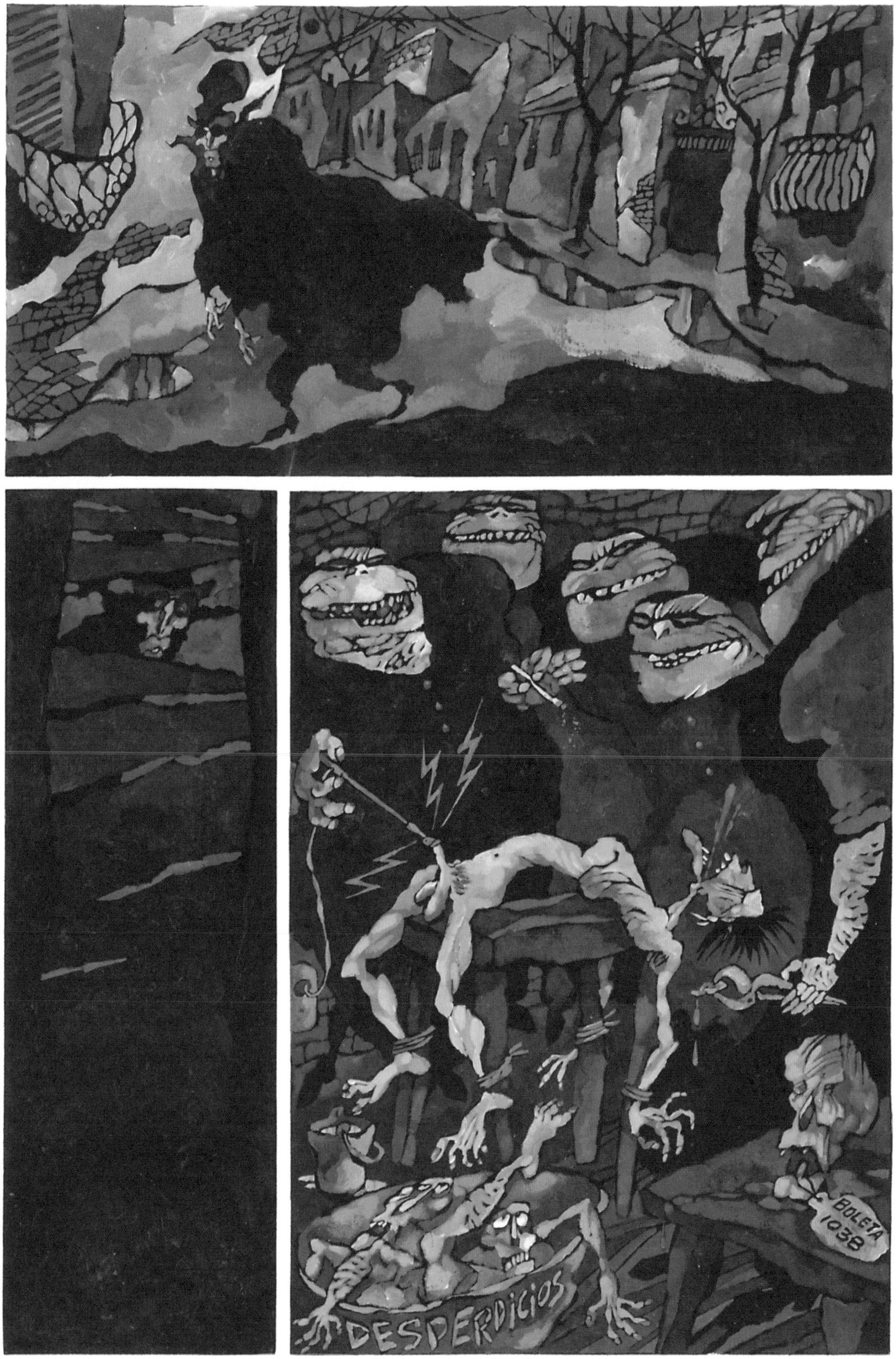
BOLETA
1038
DESPERDICIOS

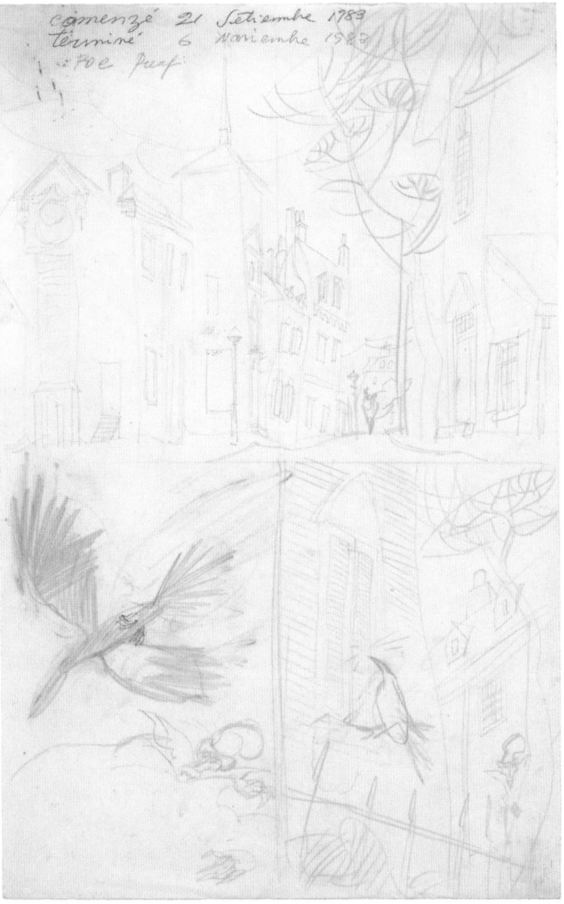
comenzé 21 Setiembre 1983
terminé 6 Noviembre 1983
Poe

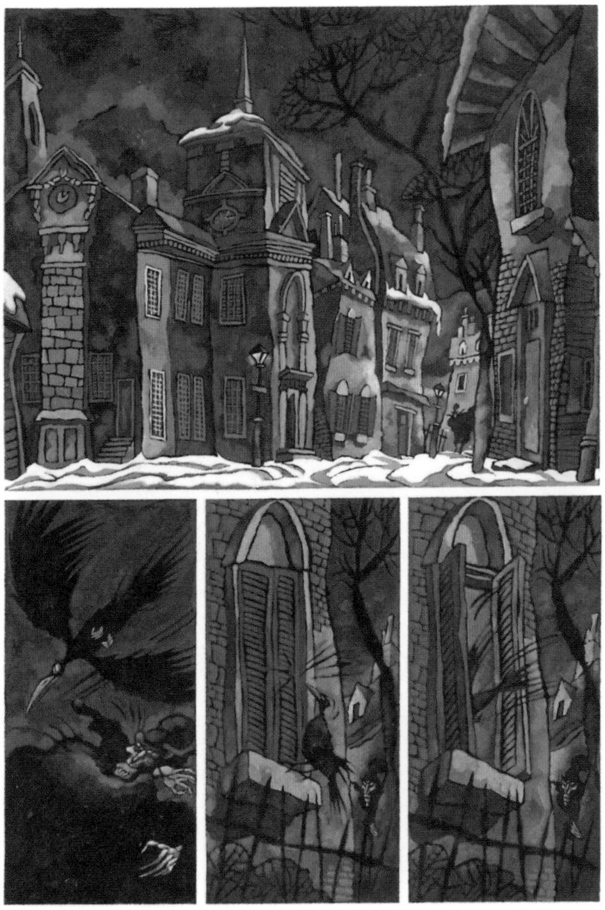

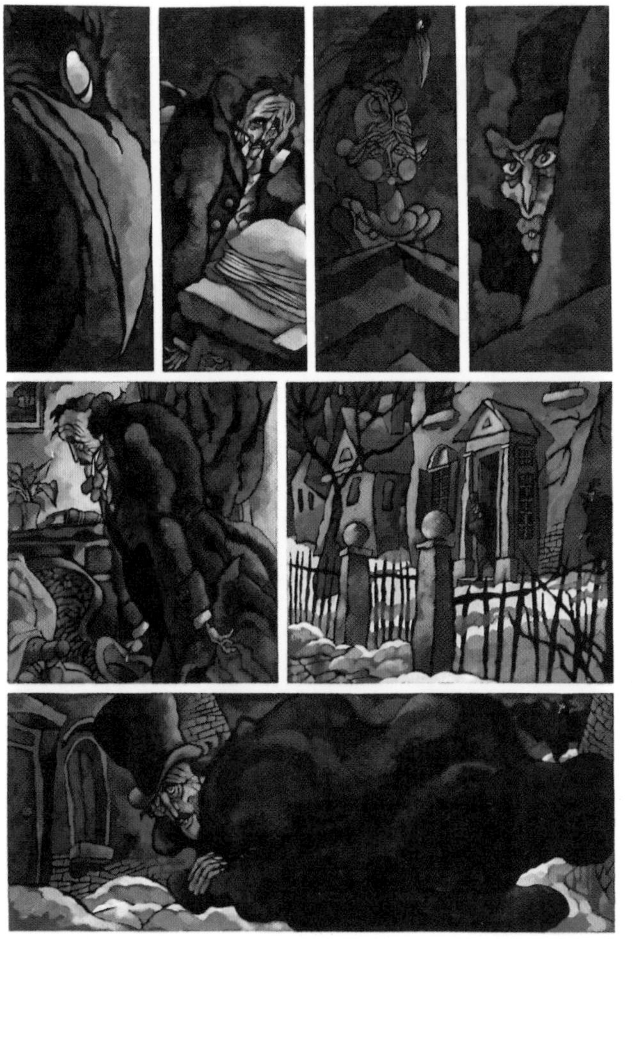

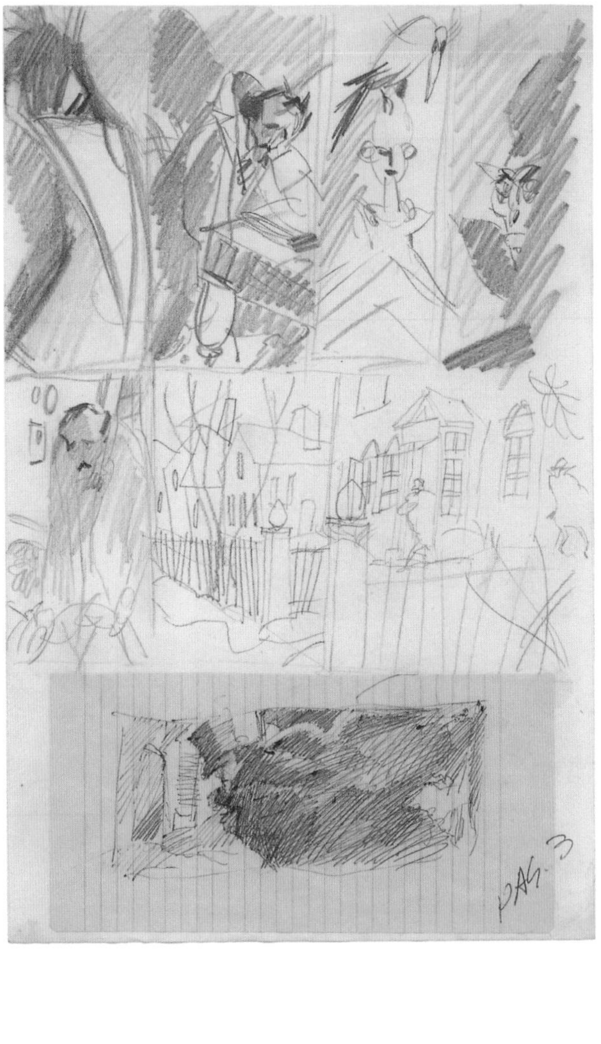
PAG. 3

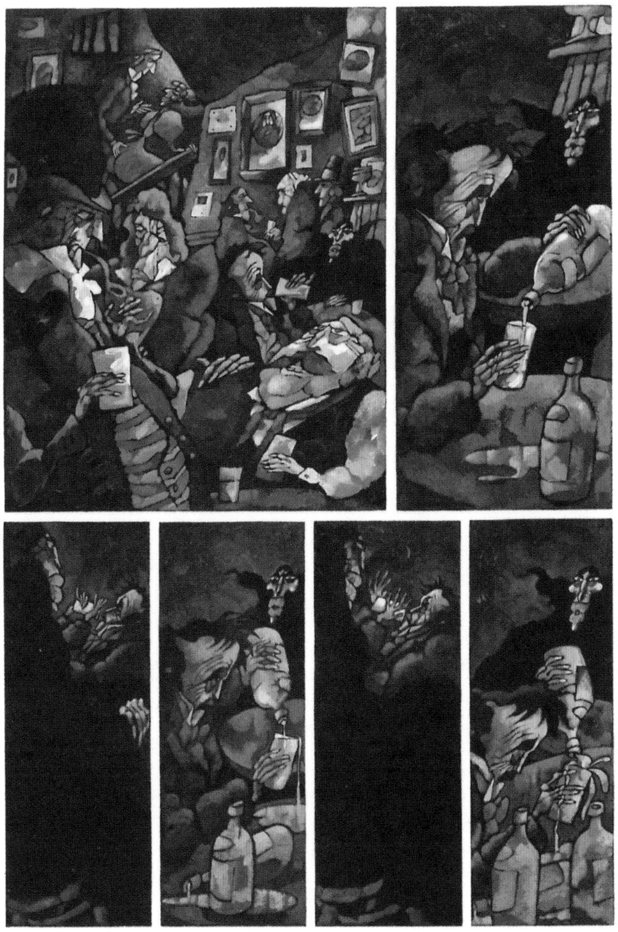

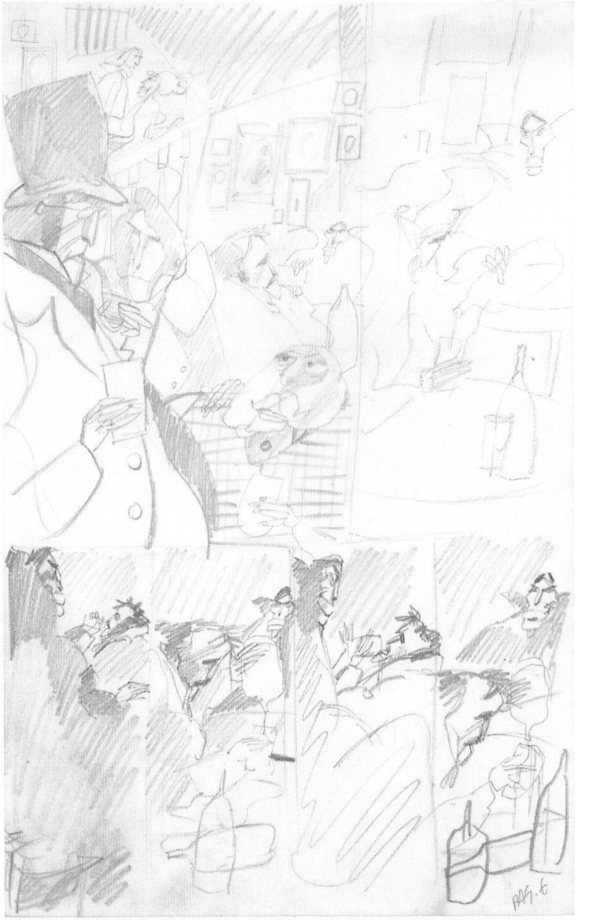
PAG. 6

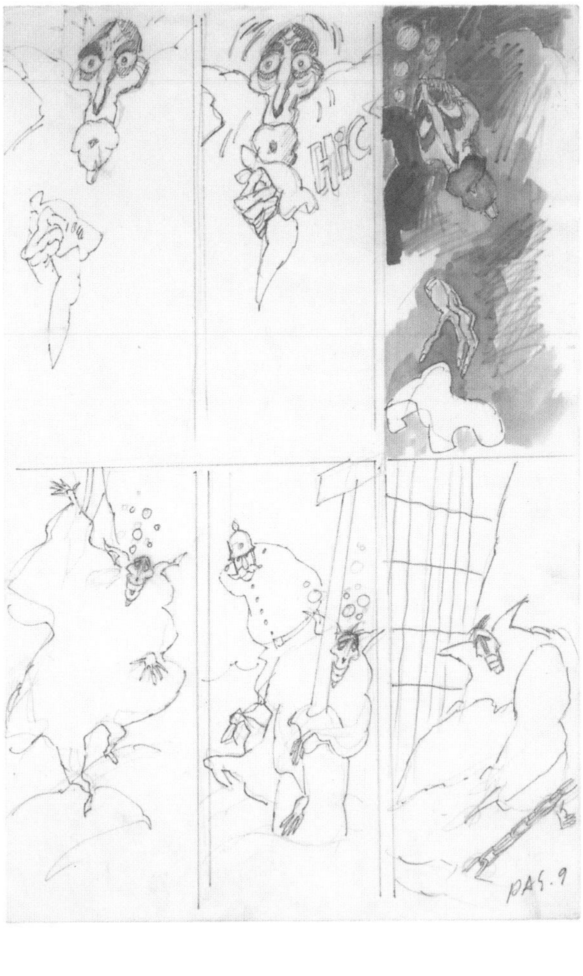
HiC
PAG. 9

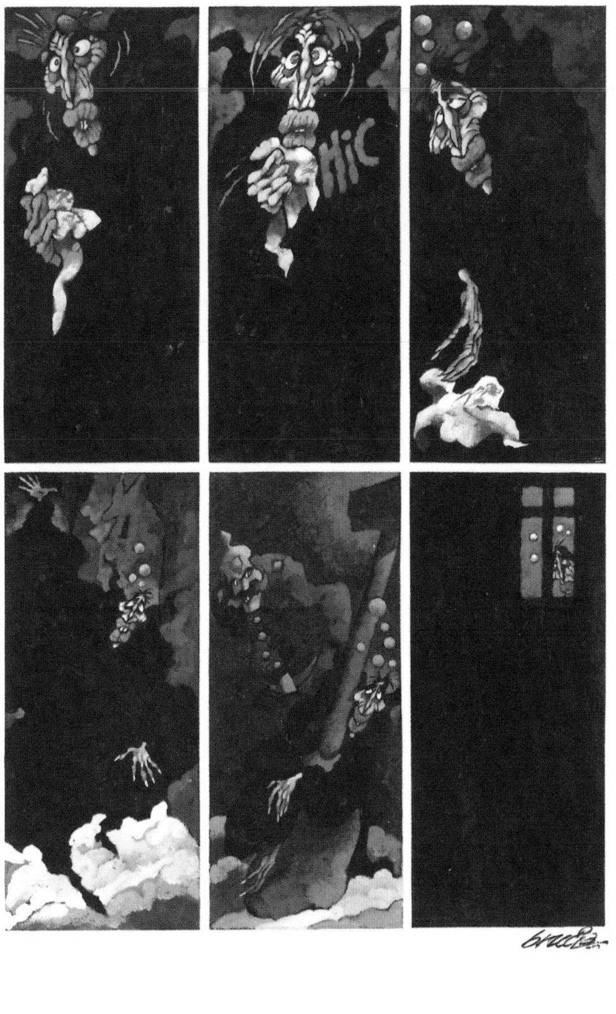
HiC

"Old Blood"

Daniele Brolli TRANSLATED BY JAMIE RICHARDS

FOR VAMPIRES, there's no avoiding blood. No matter what promises they make, no matter how much they try to skirt the subject, it is stronger than them. Everything comes down to blood. Blood is tangibly life. Yet perhaps because it performs its function hidden within the body's darkness, it quickly becomes a metaphor, even a symbol. A passing mention in a story will send readers searching for the text's deeper meaning, convinced they are reading an allegory whose significance is submerged far beneath the surface.

Alberto Breccia created his *Dracula* during the darkest days of Argentina's dictatorship, when the military junta was in decline and so all the more vicious and brutal. In that same period, in 1982, he was also drawing two comics sagas written by Carlos Trillo: *Buscavidas* (Seeking Lives) and *El viajero de gris* (The Traveler in Gray). Together, they form a trilogy, in which power is represented as a toxic, corrupt entity that, more than merely killing them, seeks to deprive people of their every intellectual asset, their identity, their liberty—the forces that give them a reason to live.

In 1980, General Roberto Viola succeeded Jorge Rafael Videla, taking brutal measures to allay the hemorrhage of inflation. Viola promised free elections by 1983, but Argentina's economy went into free fall, and, in December 1981, the most extreme wing of the military establishment put a strongman in power: General Leopardi Galtieri. In a futile attempt to control the country through national pride, Galtieri launched a slapdash military campaign to occupy the Malvinas Islands. (Argentina claimed the Malvinas Islands in the mid-twentieth century and consider the British its colonizers. The British call this archipelago the Falkland Islands, and it was operating as one of their Atlantic Ocean commonwealths.) "Iron lady" Margaret Thatcher's response was swift and severe, and the English forces took back the islands after air and naval skirmishes cost the lives of thousands of Argentines. In deference to the tribal belief that misfortune is overcome by sacrifice, defeat marked Galtieri's end, and in July 1982 he was succeeded by General Reynaldo Bignone, who took over Viola's program and restored constitutional law. In October 1983, they held the promised elections, which resulted in the victory of Raúl Alfonsín.

Alfonsín put together an investigatory committee to locate the thousands of disappeared dissidents, *los desaparecidos*; many were killed, drowned in the Atlantic. He purged the upper ranks of the army and secret service; repealed Bignone's decree of amnesty for the perpetrators of excessive violence; and sent many high-ranking officials to the military court, including the entire presidential line from 1976 to 1983. And the trial against the generals concluded with apparently severe sentences that were eventually reduced in 1986 and 1987, respectively. The "Punto Final" (Full Stop) and "Obediencia Debida" (Due Obedience) laws granted amnesty for the military juntas' political crimes; and absolved everyone who, as subordinates, claimed to have acted on orders from above. Economic recovery remained difficult, triggering social tensions that facilitated other problematic situations, but that's another story . . .

In 1982, Alberto Breccia was a political target. Anyone who used their brain, as he once put it in an interview, was suspect. All it took was finding clippings of author reviews and books someone wanted to read during a bus search—as was his situation—to wind up on some list, which gave the impression that they were hiding who knows what. In any case, with all its cruelty, the Argentine regime realized that anyone who did intellectual work couldn't help but feel the urge to rebel. During that period, Breccia received numerous death threats, telephone calls with promises to blow up his house and kill him. Are comics subversive enough to concern the establishment? Indeed, comics been enormously popular in Argentina since the 1950s. Their creators were considered bona fide stars and influential thinkers, and as such, presented a danger. And the works that Breccia created openly challenged the regime.

His Dracula is grotesque, far from the romantic allure of the character from Bram Stoker's 1897 novel—and even further from the Romanian fifteenth-century prince Vlad II, also known as "Dracul" ("devil," in the modern language) due to his ferocious and bloody offense against the Ottomans. Instead, Breccia's is an almost-humorous character, runty and sympathetic. But he's coated in color, like a kind of greasepaint. It covers up a more hazardous substance, as exposed in these enclosed preparatory sketches that so resemble the mordant satire (and style) of George Grosz or Oskar Kokoschka. For some Argentines, this Dracula might call to mind Thomas Polgar, the elusive Hungarian-born international spy who, during his service for the Argentine regime (and the CIA), was the star of a few wild and grotesque events. But this too is another story.

The subject matter of these stories is evident and identifiable in every episode. The vulnerable are the first to be swayed by their persecutors, the first to yield to the populist seduction of their power; in time, dictatorship eventually self-destructs and strengthens its victims' conscience (and resistance). Dictatorship ends up feeding itself to its victims to ensure their survival: i.e., dictators, believing their victims to demonstrate devotion and love through total self-sacrifice, accept the partial sacrifice of themselves to sustain the system. Each new regime distinguishes itself from its predecessor with increasingly harsh methods of repression; dictatorship's evolution is its barbarization; the dictator no longer lives his own life but absorbs that of his victims, suffering their same anguish. Yet Breccia's true insight into this era concerns state violence. The old vampire mocks the regime, playing both the role of the (ridiculous) butcher and the disoriented victim of a world that is transforming too quickly for someone from an epoch of feudal holdovers. We too often forget that Argentina gave asylum to Nazi officials fleeing the regime in exchange for gold. And that act sowed the seeds. A boorish and antiquated latifundismo based purely on the exploitation of labor, supported by the advantage of inherited wealth, continued to play its role by inertia, and contracted that deadly virus brought by the Europeans, analogous to the fate of the indigenous people with the conquistadors.

This is how most of the population succumbed, failing to recognize the advent of a new reality: they were variously rich, middle-class, and especially working class, while some members of the most privileged classes who had joined the new cause for power were in cahoots with the military. They confiscated, killed, stole. The military juntas that cracked down one after the other in the name of the need to eradicate communism from society, managing and hiding wealth, became the middlemen of a new reality. In the episode "I Was Legend," *Alberto Breccia's Dracula* describes the turnover of an aristocratic feudal entity that lives on the work of the subjugated classes by means of a parasitic system (the vampire) to a butcher who simply keeps the population alive because he considers them a herd of animals at pasture to be slaughtered for his own nutritional needs.

It is the portrait of a people who, in Breccia's vision, seem to have no hope of eluding the slow and irrevocable twilight of reason.

DANIELE BROLLI is an Italian comics artist, writer, editor, and publisher. **JAMIE RICHARDS** is an Italian-to-English translator from Southern California currently living in Milan, Italy.

ALBERTO BRECCIA was born in Montevideo, Uruguay, in 1919. When he was three, he moved to Buenos Aires, Argentina. At a young age, he worked in a slaughterhouse. But he was soon part of Argentina's "golden age" of comics, which began in the '40s, and for which he drew dozens of pages per week—mostly in the action, adventure, humor, or film adaptation genres. In addition, he did commercial artwork for advertising and children's books. In 1946, he began to draw his first recognizable character, Vito Nervio, (written by Leonardo Wadel). There were glimmers of it beforehand, but with this character, Breccia's personal style came to the surface. In 1958, he collaborated for the first time with scriptwriter Héctor Germán Oesterheld (HGO), on *Sherlock Time*, and his graphic art cohered and darkened. He delivered lots of Westerns and war comics to Europe, but the turning point in his career arrived in 1962, when he collaborated with HGO on *Mort Cinder*, a masterpiece of narrative, drawing, and graphic experimentation, published serially in the Argentine magazine *Misterix* until 1964.

Breccia in Paris in 1987. Photo courtesy of the Breccia estate.

In debt, with three children and a sick wife, Breccia abandoned comics for several years and dedicated himself to teaching at the Panamerican School of Art and IDA-Institute of Art Directors. During that time, he only completed the three-page comic "Richard Long" (which Oesterheld also wrote), continuing his graphic experiments by means of collage. One of the first times Breccia was recognized as an *auteur* came shortly afterward in an essay by Argentine intellectual Oscar Masotta, co-director of the World Comics Biennial. (The Biennial was held in 1968 at the Di Tella Institute, the heart of Buenos Aires's pop art scene at that time.)

The year 1968 also marked Breccia's return to comics, once again via stories written by Oesterheld. Together, they completed the surprisingly contemporary *La Vida de Che* (it also had sequences drawn by his son, Enrique Breccia) and a retelling of Oesterheld's seminal *The Eternaut*, published weekly in—oddly—a gossip magazine. Times were not the same as when Oesterheld wrote the original version (in 1957, drawn by Francisco Solano López). As dictatorships became more frequent and bloody all over the world, events led HGO to change a central detail in the script: in this new version, the great world powers hand Latin America over to the invaders… and Breccia's graphic innovations became even more psychedelic. Readers considered it "inexplicable" and "confusing," so Oesterheld himself shortened the script to quickly complete its publication. The following year, they collaborated on *The Life and Work of Eva Perón: A*

Graphic History. Both this and *Che* were controversial because of political figures they depicted and—due to persecution by successive Argentine dictatorships—their original pages and hard copies of the graphic novels disappeared. They were confiscated or lost.

The beginning of the '70s meant recognition in Europe for Breccia: much of his work was republished in books and magazines, and he was invited to and given awards at comics festivals and conventions. From that moment on, he stopped making commissioned comics to become "a professional who dedicates the required time" to comics and started to "feel the joy of drawing in another way," according to *Breccia, El Viejo: Conversations with Juan Sasturain*.

He worked with writers such as Carlos Trillo, Guillermo Saccomanno, Juan Sasturain, and Norberto Buscaglia on original scripts; he also adapted tales by Edgar Allan Poe, H. P. Lovecraft, W. W. Jacobs, the Brothers Grimm, Lord Dunsany, and the Latin Americans Horacio Quiroga, Jorge Luis Borges, Gabriel García Márquez, Juan Rulfo, Juan Carlos Onetti, Alejo Carpentier, and João Guimarães Rosa.

With his expertise, Breccia was able to take advantage of the short story comics form and innovate, narrate, and experiment without repeating himself. Breccia also drew long-running series like *Nadie* [Nobody] (1997), *El Viajero de Gris* [The Gray Traveler] (1978), *Buscavidas* [Seeking Lives] (1981), *Drácula, Dacul, Vlad?, Bah…* (1984), and *El Dorado: el delirio de Lope de Aguirre* [El Dorado: Lope de Aguirre's Delirium] (1992). The four-volume series *Perramus*, which Sasturain wrote, was recognized in 1989 by Amnesty International. *Report on the Blind*, an excerpt adapted from Ernesto Sábato's classic novel, *On Heroes and Tombs*, was published during Breccia's final year. He had resumed teaching dozens of students who valued new and personal aesthetics. Cancer metastasized and carried Breccia away on November 10, 1993, just when, in Argentina, Cartoonist Day is commemorated.

Ezequiel Garcia is an Argentine artist born in 1975. After studying under Alberto Breccia, Garcia co-edited several comics anthologies and has had short works appear in comics magazines in Europe and South America. In 2000, he was given the comics award at the Salão del Humor de Piraci-caba in Brazil. Garcia's first graphic novel, *Turning 30*, was released in Argentina in 2007. More recently, Garcia has served as a comics teacher, art gallery curator, and co-organizer of the Festival Increible de Historietas, Fanzines y Afines. Fantagraphics published his graphic novel, *Growing Up in Public*, in the U.S. in 2016. Further updates can be found at www.ezequielgarcia.com.ar.

Next Time

In the 1960s, Héctor Germán Oesterheld and Breccia were commissioned to create a graphic biography. Alberto's son, Enrique, assisted with the art. Their comic about Ernesto Guevara, *Life of Che,* came out only three months after the Argentine revolutionary's death and was instantly popular with readers. In the 1970s, the military junta banned the book and attempted to destroy the means to reprint it. Fantagraphics is proud to present *Life of Che* in English for the first time.

PUBLICATION HISTORY

Alberto Breccia wrote and drew these stories circa 1983. He began thumbnailing "The Last Night of Carnival" in February 1983 (see the sketchbook in this volume for a peek at his process) and labeled his last set of preparatory drawings as finished in November 1983—the general election on October 30 marked the end of a series of military dictatorships in Argentina.

At that time, in the Western world, the European market was the only place for literary comics aimed at adults. And so these five tales were serialized in Spain, in the monthly magazine *Comix Internacional*, nos. 45–49 (September 1984–February 1985). True to its name, *International Comics* ran installments of comics from different countries: so *Alberto Breccia's Dracula* appeared alongside Franco-Belgian work, American independent titles, and more.

EDITOR: Kristy Valenti
SUPERVISING EDITOR: Gary Groth
DESIGNER: Jacob Covey
PRODUCTION:
    Christina Hwang and Paul Baresh
ASSOCIATE PUBLISHER: Eric Reynolds
PUBLICITY: Jacq Cohen
PUBLISHER: Gary Groth

Special thanks to Latino Imparato at Rackham Editions for his generous help.

Alberto Breccia's Dracula (Vol. 4 of The Alberto Breccia Library) is copyright

© 2021 Alberto Breccia. This edition copyright © 2021 Fantagraphics Books, Inc. Afterword: "Old Blood" copyright © 2021 Daniele Brolli. Afterword translation copyright © 2021 Jamie Richards. Alberto Breccia biography copyright © 2021 Ezequiel García. All text and images are copyright their respective copyright owners. All rights reserved.

Permission to quote or reproduce material for reviews must be obtained from the publisher.

Fantagraphics Books, Inc. 7563 Lake City Way NE, Seattle, WA 98115 (800) 657-1100 www.fantagraphics.com.

Follow us on Twitter and Instagram @fantagraphics and on Facebook at Facebook.com/Fantagraphics.

ISBN: 978-1-68396-439-1
Library of Congress Control Number: 2020949183
First Edition: 2021
Printed in China